I0463389

Dialogue & Initiative

2014 Edition

Strategy, Austerity, War and the Right

Published by the
Committees of Correspondence Education Fund

Changemaker Publications

Dialogue & Initiative is a discussion journal published by the Committees of Correspondence Education Find, Inc.,

220 E. 42nd St, #407, New York, NY 10017.

(212) 868-3773

Email: national@cc-ds.org
Web: www.cc-ds.org

Editor: Harry Targ

Editorial Committee: Carl Bloice (1939-2014), Pat Fry, Michael Kaufman,Ted Pearson, Ted Reich, Meta Van Sickle

Layout and design for this issue: Carl Davidson,

Manuscripts not exceeding 5000 words are invited. Send text via email; hard copy can be mailed or faxed. Manuscripts will be returned if a acompanied by postage-paid, self-addressed packaging.

ISBN# 978-1-312-21139-1

Order online direct at:
http://www.lulu.com/spotlight/changemaker

Carl Bloice

January 28, 1939 - April 12, 2014

This issue of *Dialogue & Initiative* is dedicated to the memory and work of founding co-editor Carl Bloice, life-long working class journalist, political theorist, internationalist, leader and teacher.   *D&I* was launched with the founding of the Committees of Correspondence for Democracy and Socialism in 1992, the organization that Carl co-chaired and gave leadership to until his last days. Carl will be remembered for his unrelenting attention to struggle against inequality and joblessness, war and austerity. In his writings for *D&I*, and numerous publications over decades including the *Black Commentator, Portside, Foreign Policy in Focus, Black Scholar, People's World, People's Daily World*, and as editor of the California Nurses Association magazine, Carl gave voice to the struggles of working people everywhere. His body of work will be marked in history for the present and future.

Carl Bloice, Presente!

Table of Contents

Introduction

The Deepening Economic Crisis and Growing Resistance

The crises of capitalism and basic survival of humankind continue to deepen. At the same time, reports from various places in the United States and around the world suggest that popular resistance to finance and monopoly capital and the pain and suffering it causes on a day-to-day basis is growing as well.

The 2014 issue of *Dialogue and Initiative* opens with essays that address the worsening crisis of capitalism and what it means for working people all across the globe. Essays by Bloice, Williamson, Davis, and Johnson both analyze the development of capitalism as a system and reflect on its most recent incarnation. Central to the essays is an understanding of the intricate connections between class, race, and gender.

The second section of the D and I offers descriptions of several of the most recent forms of resistance. Particular attention is given to growing fight backs in the U.S. South, the so-called Moral Mondays movement, and how growing multi-issue progressive campaigns are spreading all across the nation. Essays in this section also raise important questions about how elections relate to growing resistance and the imperative of incorporating eco-socialism into our thinking and action.

Finally, three essays address some of the changes occurring in the international system-the economic reforms in China, the condition of the left in Europe, and the connections between the far rightwing in the United States and U.S. covert campaigns to destabilize and overthrow regimes overseas.

The ideas embedded in this issue of *Dialogue and Initiative* are a work in progress as are our mobilizations to create a more just and humane world.

—*Dialogue and Initiative Editorial Committee*

Take a Free Subscription to Our Weekly E-Newsletter...

Easy to sign on and to unsubscribe as well. Go to http://tinyurl.com.ccdslinks, pick a back issue, and click the button in the left column. Arrives every Friday AM

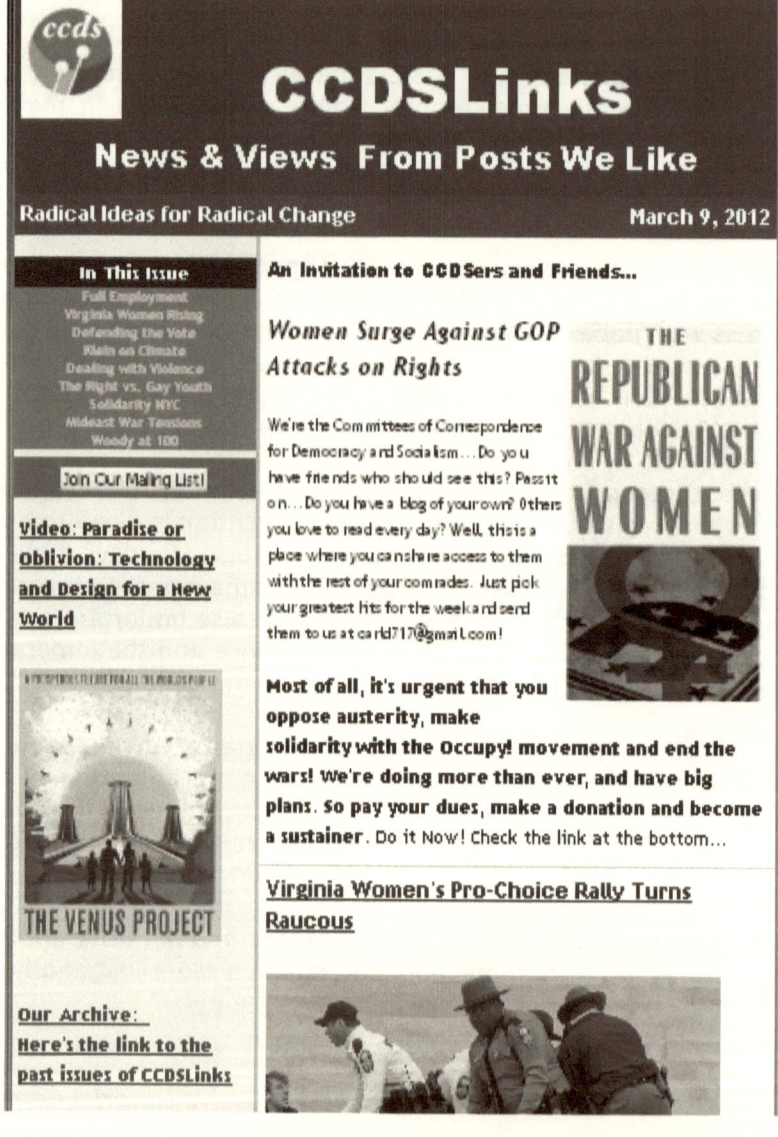

Part One: The Time of Day

A Challenge for the Left: Unite & Defeat Austerity

Carl Bloice, founding leader and National Co-Chair of the Commit-tees of Correspondence for Democracy and Socialism, authored the following remarks delivered July 17, 2013 at the CCDS 7th National Convention in Pittsburgh, PA. Addressing the essential basis of unity of the socialist left in defense of working people today, this was Carl's last formal presentation. He died April 12, 2014 in San Francisco from a long battle with cancer. Carl's message here is representative of his life-long commitment to the struggle against inequality and de-fense of working people everywhere. Carl Bloice, Presente!

By Carl Bloice

The argument for a new form of left unity in our country based on our respective or-ganizations' relatively small numbers and the potential value of pooling our limited resources is a compelling one. As is the contention that whatever differences ex-ist today amongst us are mostly about the past and it would be a good thing to keep the discussion going on evaluation of the socialist movement's history in the U.S. and worldwide while at the same time concentrating our efforts on meeting the political chal-lenges of the day. I am convinced that the effort to achieve such unity is possible if we maintain an atmosphere of tolerance and eschew subjective responses to past encounters and disputes.

However, I am equally certain that such an effort will fail if it is pre-mised on combining our numbers alone or if we fail to collectively define the nature of today's primary challenges and agreement on our objectives in the immediate period ahead. I would argue that the central tasks of the left today are the struggle for democracy and the defense of working people in the face of the onslaught by those who benefit the most from contemporary capitalism.

This effort should involve not only members of existing socialist groups and publications but the many unorganized left activists in the struggle for economic and social justice, democracy and peace.

A strategy has been put in place in the upper echelons of the system to deal with and resolve the crisis of the current economic system by preserving the wealth and prerogatives of the privileged and exploiters, by forcing working women and men and their families to accept a smaller share of the wealth produced in the economy and therefore a lower standard of living, a diminution - and in some case elimination - of social welfare guarantees acquired by working people over centuries of struggle.

Unrestricted Inequity

This entails moves to eliminate any semblance of economic democracy including the right to organize and confront capital collectively. It involves guaranteeing the right of capital to operate unrestricted across the planet without regard for the safety or welfare of working people while restricting the right of working people to move across borders in search of a means to earn a living. It means preservation of a system involving the maintenance of gross economic and social inequities between ethnic and racial groups and between men and women. It means the promotion of a two-tiered education system that further entrenches class and racial divisions.

This class warfare involves preservation of a system that seeks only short term economic gains for the one-percent. It is oblivious to the threat this entails for the health of the biosphere and the preservation of life on the planet. It ignores the fact that the immediate effect of climate change falls most heavily on the communities of the less fortunate.

Call it "austerity" or its larger more systemic designation "neo-liberalism," this class warfare is a major element in the massive upsurges today in countries and regions across the globe.

Everywhere people on the left are aware that the root of this campaign is traceable to the effort to salvage capitalism in the midst of crisis and that the world needs more socialism. I would argue that the path ahead must lead in that direction and that the key to the growth and increased influence and relevance of the socialist left lies in unity in action in defense of democracy and the well-being of working people everywhere. This must involve the day to day and militant defense of social programs such as Social Security, Medicare, food and housing assistance, aid to needy children, Head Start and environmental protection.

Moreover, a program of a united left must offer an alternative view of politics and economics; one that encompasses greater economic democracy, advancement of the true interests of the 99 percent and an equitable sharing of the wealth of nations. It would require a lot of hard work, and debate and exploration that cannot be accomplished in one day but we can do it, together.

What Time of Day is It? No Respect for Humanity: Economic, Social, Environmental, Racial Injustice on Steroids

The following presentation by Mildred Williamson, a founding leader of the Committees of Correspondence for Democracy and Socialism, was delivered at the CCDS 7th National Convention, July 17, 2013 in Pittsburgh, PA. Her remarks below address the crisis confronting the entire working class, the particular issues confronting Black and Brown people, and the challenge for the Left.

By Mildred Williamson

The unemployment rate is 9.3% (double or higher for Black people in certain communities); yet bourgeois economists and political pundits still characterize today's economy as in "recovery."

Mega-banks, now bigger and more profitable today than prior to the 2007-2008 meltdown, are bailed out while millions of people, including renters, remain devastated by foreclosures with too little or no help from government or lenders. And while the foreclosure tragedy has affected people of every nationality, the impact of foreclosure on black communities has virtually served to wipe out what little "wealth" that had been acquired. The income and wealth inequality gap is now something not seen of this magnitude since slavery.

In fact, how far can we say we have we come from the "3/5ths of a man," the constitutional definition of how black people should be considered in U.S. society? I say - not far enough and if there is no sustained, organized struggle, witness the Supreme Court decision on the Voting Rights Act, we will see an accelerated march backwards away from social progress. In the aftermath of the Zimmerman trial, some observers have noted that Philadelphia Eagles' quarterback Michael Vick served time in prison for organizing dog fights that resulted in death and injury to animals. However, George Zimmerman and countless numbers of official law enforcement officers throughout the U.S. have shot and killed numerous human beings who happen to be people of color, including unarmed youth like Trayvon Martin; yet, they have not been convicted, served time, lost pay or prestige in their positions of power over our lives.

Lest we not forget the hundreds, thousands of persons are incarcerated for crimes they did not commit. Even those with evidence of committing criminal acts, the high percentage convicted is the result of an unjust war on drugs that translates as a war on black and brown life, especially youth. Many have died in prisons of preventable causes, due to less-than-standard of care provided in many cases, by for-profit correctional health care providers.

Public education is crumbling and living wage jobs are scarce, even for many with college educations. The role and proliferation of privatized pre-school, K-12 and proprietary higher education institutions are essentially ensuring that working class people with aspirations of improving their lives will have obstacles that may be insurmountable to overcome, due to profit-making at all costs, trumping everything - even human life.

Battle over schools

In Chicago, were it not for the solid labor-community-student-parent coalition built with leadership from the Chicago Teachers Union, people around the country would not have known about the vicious scheme of Mayor Rahm Emanuel to close more than 100 schools that through fightback, got reduced to less than 50 - still the most closures in the history of this country. Stay tuned for the outcome of the two lawsuits pending, one based on racial discrimination (80% African American and Latino children affected), and the other based on 30% of students with disabilities and special needs affected by the closings.

What time of day is it? Here is the answer from the Grandmother of NAACP Executive Director Ben Jealous in response to many of his young Black friends' fears that they will not live long enough to reach their 21st birthdays: Jealous said to his grandmother, our generation of black Americans was supposed to be the first not to be judged by our race or the color of our skin. Instead, we came of age to find ourselves the most incarcerated on the planet and most murdered in the country. "Grandma," Jealous would ask days later still searching for understanding: "What happened? How did things turn out like this?"

Her response was the crux of his speech to the 104th NAACP convention in July 2013. "She leaned in," he said, "and spoke softly: 'It's sad but it's simple: We got what we fought for, but we lost what we had.'"

Did we really get all of what we fought for - or was it derailed by:

- the impact of the Smith Act, McCarran Act, Right to Work laws?
- the blacklisting, imprisonment, deportation and murder of radicals and communists, particularly the purge from labor and other social justice organizations?
- the assassination of Dr. Martin Luther King, Medgar Evers, Malcolm X, Fred Hampton and many others?
- COINTELPERO?
- the de-industrialization and global outsourcing of unionized, living wage, manufacturing jobs?
- the Nixon-led Southern Strategy, virtually unchecked, followed by the Reagan right wing surge?
- the war on drugs and mass incarceration?
- the "No Child Left Behind" and "Race to the Top?"
- the Vietnam war, the wars in Iraq and Afghanistan, Gulf Wars I and II?

Each of these policies and events served a purpose for the ruling class - to weaken or squash over time radical thought and action for multiracial working class power and the struggle to affirm value in black and brown life - the right to fulfill our human potential. Though there have been extraordinary victories in the struggle for social justice, ending wars in Vietnam and Iraq, brilliant victories in numerous key elections, some union organizing successes, freedom of many political prisoners, starting with Angela Davis - we still remain challenged by getting the intertwining issues of class-race-gender right in our strategy and tactics of struggle on every issue from jobs to healthcare, immigration, incarceration, the environment and climate change. Our ability to make and sustain social progress critically depends on this. Disciplined, organized, radical leadership is essential to move us forward.

I am encouraged by the recent demonstrations of numerous low-wage workers fighting for a living wage - McDonald's, Wal-Mart, even Foot Locker workers. Some of these have taken place in Chicago. Consider the stories of the protesters: One young black man at one of the Chicago protests reported that he worked for $10.15 an hour at a Nike store in 2008 and over 2 years he got up to $11.17 an hour. Later, the store shut down for renovations and he and his co-workers were laid off. He was called back to his same job for $10 an hour which he was still making at the time of the protest this spring 2013. This is a 5-year period of his life. He does not now, nor did he ever make enough money to live on his own - typical of most low wage, retail work.

McDonald's, just this week developed what they called a "financial planning guide" for their workers which assumes the average cost for rent at $600 per month and healthcare at $20 per month, and a second job in addition to their full time McDonald's job netting an average $24,000 yearly wage to make ends meet. They also suggested that their workers should simultaneously be attending school to gain additional skills. This insulting plan was proposed for workers by a corporation that consistently makes super-profits, even during the recent massive recession (which is not over for many of us).

What time of day is it? As long as black and brown lives are thought of and treated as disposable in a 21st century, 3/5th of a person fashion, it will be impossible to achieve working class power in this country.

Attacks on People of Color Weaken Everyone

Economic and social policies are literally destroying black and brown lives, and simultaneously weakening working class power. Case in point: Former President George W. Bush once called a meeting at the White House with members of the Congressional Black Caucus. In an effort to persuade them to support his proposal to essentially privatize Social Security he shared that the CBC should support this idea because he said Social Security was unfair to African Americans. Why? Because, he said, the life expectancy for black workers was shorter and therefore received an average of $21,000 less in benefits than whites of comparable income levels. He said personal accounts such as a 401k plan could be passed along to the next generation, and would go a long way toward reducing that disparity. (Source: Decision Points, by Pres. George W. Bush, p.298-299, Nov 9, 2010)

Instead of addressing the socio-economic determinants of why black life expectancy is shorter than other groups in the U.S., then President G.W. Bush cynically told his Congressional Black Caucus guests that it is better to just save up on your own into a plan that is beholden to the ups and downs of the stock market. How insulting it must have been for these Congressional leaders to sit there and hear that - just as it remains insulting for Cong. John Lewis and all other living participants of the civil rights movement to hear the Supreme Court decision to virtually butcher the Voters Rights Act.

To achieve comprehensive social change that shifts the balance of power toward the working class, it is essential to reject white supremacy and embrace all disenfranchised elements of humanity. This requires radical, disciplined leadership that is disciplined in thought and purpose to build a movement anchored by the voice and action of organized and unorganized workers and marginalized populations. The labor movement has the right slogan - Jobs with Justice. We need both - not either/ or. Though the labor movement is at its smallest in size, that which remains, must continue and grow its coalition with others for a significant rise in the minimum wage, for massive reinvestment in public education for all, for LGBTQ rights, for the right of women to all aspects of reproductive health and freedom from abuse, for the rights of immigrants, for the right to quality public education including higher education, for the abolishment of prisons and an overhaul of the criminal justice system - and for ending all modern vestiges of slavery, Jim Crow and genocide in institutions and in human interaction.

Finally, we must fight with humility and purpose to strengthen and promote radicalized thought and action in the quest for social justice, human rights and working class power. This requires a fresh look at what it means to be "Left" in this phase of capitalism. What is the winning strategy to reduce the number of white working class folks from voting against their own class interests, especially since fewer are unionized and even fewer live in integrated communities? What will be the winning strategy to achieve left unity - and what does that mean? How can we build respect for youth in leadership of social justice movements while still showing simultaneous respect for elders? How do we fully move our thought and action from the multi-racial unity slogan to normalized, genuine demonstration of respect for multiple cultures, gender expressions and sexual orientation? These questions and more tough ones need answers in order to chart the path forward in the quest for working class power.

Black History: Understanding and Challenging Racism Today

The following address by Prof. Angela Y. Davis was delivered at the Black History Month program organized by the Communist Party USA in New York City on February 26, 2014. Internationally renowned author and activist Angela Y. Davis is Distinguished Professor Emerita of History of Consciousness and Feminist Studies at the University of California, Santa Cruz. The address is reprinted with permission of Prof. Davis.

By Angela Y. Davis

Thank you for inviting me to join you in celebrating Black History Month. I was asked specifically to speak about the importance of understanding and challenging racism, especially within the context of the damage wrought by the emboldened conservative forces in this country.

Racism has played a central role in shaping this country's economic, political, and social histories. There are those who assume that the triumph of the civil rights movement was equivalent to purging the country of racism. In other words, the dismantling of the legal structures of racism is often assumed to be the end of racism, per se. The legal doctrine of colorblindness is often represented as the ultimate triumph over racism, as the election of Barack Obama is represented as the ultimate defeat of racism in the U.S. And of course, if these assumptions are true, we must now be in a post-racial era.

But it seems that the very presence of a black president in Washington has unleashed countless instances of the overt racism that many of us had thought had been put to rest - not only the racisms with which we are familiar, but also relatively new instantiations of racism - the vicious anti-Muslim racism, for example, that is so characteristic of the post 9/11 era.

We have come together on the 2nd anniversary of the killing of Trayvon Martin at a time when demonstrations and marches are taking place here in New York and all over the country. These observances mark much more than life of a single individual. However important Trayvon's life may have been, what we are opposed to is systematic racist violence. We can see this racism unfolding within the context of the unjust incarceration of Marisa Alexander in Florida, and in the way the killing of Jordan Davis for playing loud music has been handled in that state. In North Carolina Jonathan Ferrell, who was attempting to get help after having sustained an automobile accident, was shot by the police. Countless instances of racist violence can still be identified, not because racism and violence are natural human phenomena and will always be with us (which is what the state would like us to assume), but rather because of the structural racism that has not been fundamentally troubled since the era of slavery. In fact we can say that even as legal institutions of racism have been dismantled, structural racism has become even more strongly embedded in the economic, educational, correctional and health care institutions of this country.

Triple Danger: Racism, Militarism, Capitalism

We should never underestimate the importance of the mid-twentieth century civil rights struggles, but the triumph of civil rights was not the end of racism. Even Dr. King came to acknowledge what he called the triple dangers of racism, militarism and what he called materialism, but I think this was a euphemism for capitalism. So we can say racism, militarism and capitalism.

W.E.B. Dubois wrote the monumental work *"Black Reconstruction in America"* in 1935. Eric Williams wrote *"Capitalism and Slavery"* in 1944, but there are still those who try to resist the implications of this link between capitalism and slavery for our world today.

This is Black History Month. What is the meaning of black history? Not long ago, I spoke at an elementary school in Oakland. I always try to visit classrooms during Black History Month. The kids in this particular class immediately began to ask me questions about black historical figures I may have met. "Did you know Dr. Martin Luther King?" one asked. I said in response, "I actually met him on several occasions." And then another asked, "Did you know Malcolm X? Did you know Rosa Parks?," both of whom I had also met. And then someone asked, "Did you know Harriet Tubman?" (laughter). This was a fourth grade class. I said, "No, I didn't know her and does anyone know why I could not have met her in person?" A young Latino boy raised his hand and said, "Yes, because Harriet Tubman died in 1913." That was really quite impressive. Later, I thought maybe I should have said that I did know her because the whole point I was trying to make was that our histories are still with us. Histories should not to be so fully relegated to the past that we forget how they have helped to produce what we experience as the present.

The core meaning of black history is the quest for freedom. And this is why black history is relevant to everyone regardless of racial or ethnic or national backgrounds. It is not only the yearning for freedom, but the determination to struggle for freedom - not just abstract freedoms, but substantive freedoms, i.e. jobs, living wages, health care, education, etc.

Let me say a few words about slavery. We assume that slavery was abolished in 1863. That's not quite right. Only some slaves were emancipated as a result of the issuing of the Emancipation Proclamation. Then we say, slavery came to an end in 1865 with the passage of the 13th amendment. But even if we use those markers and if we use the year 1619 as the advent of slavery in what came to be known as the United States, then that would mean that we have had at least 246 years of legalized slavery and only 149 years without slavery - one hundred more years with slavery than without.

In this context let me refer you to Douglas Blackmon's book "*Slavery By Another Name: The Re-Enslavement of Black Americans from the Civil War to World War II.*" (Doubleday, 2008) He argues that slavery did not end until the 1940s when a different form of slavery, the convict lease system, was finally abolished. So if we count that form of neo-slavery, it would mean that we have had 320 years of slavery and only about 70 years without slavery. Whichever way you look at it the majority of this country's history has been a history of slavery.

But if you consider the extent to which slavery has been relegated to a place of historical insignificance, you would never know that the majority of this country's history has unfolded under slavery. It was not some insignificant aberration. The fact that human beings were bought and sold and legally treated as property, the fact that human beings were forced to labor under the most despicable conditions, that human beings were sexually abused, that they were not recognized as human beings - this was a catastrophe that had vast implications that would influence the history, the culture, the collective psyche of this country for many, many decades to come. That there has never been a serious and consistent attempt to purge the economy, the politics, the culture and the spirit of the United States of this catastrophe has allowed it to continue to spew its damage decade after decade after decade.

The period after the constitutional abolition of slavery (which did not fully abolish slavery) from 1865 to about 1877 - a little more than a decade - was the most radical period in the history of this country. It was radical not simply in terms of efforts to roll back and challenge the consequences of racism related to slavery, but also in terms of workers' rights, and in terms of educational rights in general. White children in the South, poor white children, working class white children had never had the opportunity to get an education until black people fought for the first public education system in the South. It was a period of progressive legislation with respect to women's rights - new divorce laws, laws that allowed married women to own property, etc. We have no sense of that era. It has been completely concealed.

In his book "*Black Reconstruction*" - a book that everyone needs to read - Du Bois wrote that after the dismantling of radical reconstruction, democracy died except in the hearts of black people. The connection between the struggle against racism and the struggle for democracy in this country has always been so close that if we launch efforts to defeat racism today, we certainly have to keep these historical linkages in mind.

Jim Crow or Neo-Slavery?

Douglas Blackmon argues that we should not label the era that led up to the triumph of the civil rights movement in 1964 and 1965 as "Jim Crow." He says it actually is quite astounding that we name such a violent and racist era after a white man in black face performing on the minstrel stage. We should not call that era "Jim Crow" Blackmon argues. We should call it the "Age of Neo-Slavery" because what characterized that period more than anything else was the over-exploitation of the labor of formerly enslaved black people in ways that were often even worse than slavery.

I grew up in Birmingham, Alabama. This city was known as "the Pittsburgh of the South" because of the steel produced in Birmingham. It was a city, whose industries were iron ore, coal and steel. U.S. Steel and the Tennessee Coal, Iron and Railroad Company constructed enormous steel mills. This was the basis of the industrialization of the South which, in turn, was based on what amounted to slave labor after slavery. The punishment system that came to be called the convict lease system was an effort to manage black laboring bodies in the aftermath of the abolition of slavery.

Although quite a number of works have been written about this era, we still have no general sense of the impact of this labor system on our history. In the 1990s Milfred Fierce, who was teaching at Brooklyn College, wrote "*Slavery Revisited: Blacks and the Southern Convict Lease System, 1865-1933.*" (New York: Brooklyn College, CUNY, Africana Studies Research Center, 1994) David Oshinsky is the author of "*Worse Than Slavery: Parchman Farm and the Ordeal of Jim Crow Justice.*" (New York: The Free Press, 1996) Alex Lichtenstein produced "*Twice the Work of Free Labor: The Political Economy of Convict Labor in the New South* (Verso, 1996). And Matthew J. Mancini wrote "*One Dies, Get Another:*

Convict Leasing in the American South, 1866-1928." (Columbia, S.C.: University of South Carolina Press, 1996, p. 20.) The point that Mancini made was that at least slave owners had an investment in keeping the people alive whose labor they were exploiting, but the convict lease system did not require those who were leasing black labor to keep individual people alive. They could literally work one to death and get another one because the cost of leasing was collective and by the month. Mary Ellen Curtin's book, *Black Prisoners in Alabama* also explores this era through the letters of the people subjected to this system. Reading Blackmon, I learned that in the city where I grew up there were "slave camps" everywhere - "slave camps" adjacent to the iron ore mines, adjacent to the coal mines and adjacent to the steel mills. Slaves were the first workers at the mills. This is an important part of labor history that does not usually receive its due.

The exploitation of black labor depended on the criminalization of blackness. Laws against vagrancy were passed and laws that required black people to possess written permission before changing employers. It turns out that it was not primarily the southern racists, the old slavocracy that was responsible for the growth of this system. Rather companies like U.S. Steel and other northern capitalist concerns substantially profited from this convict labor.

Blackmon researched court records and the records of U.S. Steel, discovering that the rise in the number of people arrested directly correlated to the demand for cheap labor. U.S. Steel would announce to the local sheriffs that they needed more people to work and the sheriffs would conduct round-ups. People would be arrested for all kinds of insignificant reasons. Virtually every sheriff was involved in this process. This is one of the reasons why Southern sheriffs have always had such a bad rep, especially during the civil rights era. This is a passage from Blackmon's book:

"Instead of evidence showing black crime waves, the original records of county jails indicated thousands of arrests for inconsequential charges or for violations of laws specifically written to intimidate blacks - changing employers without permission, vagrancy, riding freight cars without a ticket, engaging in sexual activity - or loud talk - with white women. Repeatedly, the timing and scale of surges in arrests appeared more attuned to rises and dips in the need for cheap labor than any demonstrable acts of crime. Hundreds of forced labor camps came to exist...operated by state and county governments, large corporations, small-time entrepreneurs, and provincial farmers. These bulging slave centers became a primary weapon of suppression of black aspirations. Where mob violence or the Ku Klux Klan terrorized black citizens periodically, the return of forced labor as a fixture in black life ground pervasively into the lives of far more African Americans.

In Alabama alone, hundreds of pages of public documents attest to the arrests, subsequent sale and delivery of thousands of African Americans into mines, lumber camps, quarries, farms, and factories."

This helps us to understand the context for the rise of a prison-industrial complex. This history helps us to understand how it is that we have become a prison nation, and how racism and the criminalization of blackness have fueled that prison nation. It helps us to understand why the U.S. has the largest incarcerated population in the world and why such a disproportionate number of them come from racially subjugated communities.

It may no longer be the case that people are incarcerated because U.S. Steel needs cheap labor but it certainly is the case that prisoners' bodies have become extremely profitable within the context of the capitalist system, both in public prisons and in private prisons. It is still the case that it is much easier for law enforcement to harass a black person or a person of color. Racial disparities in arrests, convictions and sentences are similar to what they were during the period of what we might call Neo-Slavery. Certainly the ideological effect of the criminalization of blackness is very much with us.

Profit and Prison

As the linchpin of the prison-industrial complex, racialized mass incarceration represents the increasing profitability of punishment. It represents a global strategy of managing bodies of color, immigrant bodies and bodies perceived as immigrants no matter how many generations of people have lived here or in Europe or in Australia. The prison-industrial complex produces these bodies as surplus, disposable populations. Put them into a vast garbage bin, add sophisticated electronic technology to control them and let them languish there. In the meantime, create the ideological illusion that the surrounding society is safer and more free because all the dangerous black people are locked up.

In the meantime, corporations profit and working class and poor communities suffer. Public education suffers because it is not profitable according to corporate measures. As punishment is privatized, education for profit challenges the notion of education as a public good. Public health care suffers. If punishment can be profitable then certainly heath care should be profitable as well. If these institutions can be rendered profitable, then certainly it should be possible to profit even more from the labor of the working class.

But it is not all negative; there are also positive lessons to be gleaned from this history. From the very history of slavery and neo-slavery and the reconfigured slavery of the prison industrial complex, we learn also that resistance is not only possible but that it is the only legitimate response to these systems and apparatuses of unfreedom.

Just as we affirm connections between slavery and the prison industrial complex, we should also emphasize the link between anti-slavery abolitionism and anti-prison abolitionism. Anti-prison abolition takes up not only issues of mass incarceration, acknowledging the way race and gender structure the prison-industrial complex, but also addresses the unresolved issues such as jobs, a living wage, education, and healthcare that have been looming over our society since the dismantling of radical reconstruction in the late 19th century. We have never experienced the radical reorganization of society begun in the aftermath of slavery, but brought down by the rise of conservative forces in this country.

We are called upon to continue that struggle.

The 2008 election is still widely recognized as a world historic election. A black man was elected to the Presidency - a development that certainly exceeded our collective imagination. In my opinion, the 2012 election was far more meaningful because we learned an all-important lesson about the potential of resistance in this country. The 2012 election was not supposed to end with an Obama victory precisely because conservative Republicans had developed all kinds of voter suppression strategies all over the country. They assumed that when black voters, voters of color, poor voters discovered for example that there were only three voting booths for 5,000 people that they would simply turn around and go home. But what we saw all over the country repeatedly from one community to another was a colossal determination. In some places people waited in line for up to 12 hours, thus inviting comparisons with the first free election in South Africa that yielded a victory for Nelson Mandela.

The 2012 election taught us that it is possible to move in progressive and radical directions. This election irrefutably demonstrated that conservative white men no longer control the future of this country. (applause) Even though a majority of white men voted against Obama, this was not the case for communities of color and especially women. It was actually women who carried the 2012 election and, to be more specific, it was women of color. (applause)

Oftentimes people, particularly white people, want to be involved in anti-racist struggle but feel as if they are always implicated when we evoke slavery, and they frequently think that they are expected to feel guilty. But there is no place for guilt in radical struggles. I like what Blackmon proposes as the alternative to guilt: we all live with the inheritances of slavery. All of us, regardless of who we are, live with those inheritances. We can struggle in accordance with the ethics and politics we inherit from those who fought slavery, from those who challenged the colonization of Native Americans, and from those who fought for labor rights.

Today it is incumbent upon us to understand the intersections and interconnections that bring together a whole range of issues and struggles. If we stand up against racism, class exploitation, and heteropatriarchy we also have to challenge attacks on immigrants. The movement to defend the rights of immigrants is the civil rights movement of our time. If we stand up for immigrant rights we must also advocate for the rights of disabled people. If we believe in the rights of the disabled we must stand up against war, and torture, and militarism. If we are opposed to war, we must also be opposed to homophobia and transphobia. If we stand up for LGBTQ rights, we have to recognize how important it is to contest the violent infringement of the environment by capitalist corporations, and to challenge the way they exploit the human need for nourishment by growing GMO crops for profit and mass producing food that literally spreads illness all over the world.

While this is not an exhaustive list of contemporary movements, the very existence of such movements does remind us this is certainly the time for us to imagine and struggle for a better world for us all. Thank you very much.

An Introduction to Theory

The following is an adaptation from educational pamphlets of the South African Communist Party (SACP) and the Confederation of South African Trade Unions (COSATU) used in worker education. An improvisation written by Tim Johnson for U.S. activists, the article is based on the SACP/COSATU's Building Socialism Now: Preparing for the New Millennium and the SACP's Philosophy and Class Struggle. It is the first of a multiple-module study guide on the "Long Struggle for Democracy" organized by CCDS. The educational project has been under development for the past several months by a national group of activists and Marxist educators and will be published in the coming months.

The modules following the "Introduction to Theory" are on the Atlantic Revolutions (U.S. War of Independence, the French Revolution and the Haitian Revolution), the Civil War and Reconstruction, the Great Depression and the 1930s, the Civil Rights Movement and Post Civil Rights Movements. The final modules are on "Struggles of Today" and the "Democracy Charter," a 13 point program of substantive democracy authored by veteran civil rights strategist, Jack O'Dell, as a catalyst for discussion and mobilization in the struggle for democracy today. For information on the Democracy Charter (www.democracycharter.org) For information on the "Long Struggle for Democracy" Study Guide (national@cc-ds. org)

By Tim Johnson

This introduction attempts to give a very basic understanding of Marxism. Historically, there have been problems with getting activists in the United States to seriously engage in the study of theory and history. Firstly, we all are affected by the American philosophy of pragmatism – an attitude that solely focuses on practice to the detriment of theory. To the pragmatist, whatever works is good. This is a one-sided view of struggle. The opposite approach is reflected in those who only sit around and endlessly discuss social problems. This is also a one-sided

approach. What we strive to accomplish is a balance of theory and practice – combining theoretical study with practical activity and struggle.
Thus, Marxists often quote Lenin who stated, "There is no revolutionary movement without revolutionary theory" and Marx, who stated, "The
philosophers have only interpreted the world, the point is to change
it." These two approaches get at the necessity of wedding theory and
practice.

Those who imagine that all revolutionaries need to do is act, forget that
action on its own is not enough. (Strictly speaking, it is not even possible). No matter how passionately we hate oppression and wish to see
things change, there is only one force capable of eliminating racism,
capitalism, and reaction, and that is the oppressed masses. The organization of a popular movement around a political program able to unite
and coordinate various forms of struggle and direct them towards a
common goal is essential.

Action Has To Be Thought Out

Yet once we talk about a movement and a program, we are not simply talking about action - we are talking about action, which has been
thought out. For the only way in which anyone can plan activity and produce a program is through revolutionary thinking – the development of
revolutionary theory – which, if it is properly worked out, does not hold
back our practical activity but rather serves as a compass which enables
us to move in the direction we want to go. The more difficult and dangerous the task facing revolutionaries, the more developed and carefully
worked out their theoretical perspectives need to be.

But if we require revolutionary theory so that in Lenin's words, we can
substitute "science for dreams," why do we need a special philosophical
outlook as well? Why do we need to base our theory upon the principles
of Marxism, which is the only logical and consistent philosophy?

The construction of a theory is like the construction of a house; if it is
to stay up, then not only must the walls be sound, but also the foundations. It is to the realm of philosophy we must turn if we want to make
sure that our theory has strong foundations. For the truth is that all
theory, even if it has only been worked out in relation to one particular
problem, is rooted in philosophy, some overall view of the world. Even if
we are unaware of the existence of this underlying "world outlook," it is
there nonetheless, serving as the basis, the very foundation upon which
all thought and activity rests.

Why should this matter? It matters because in the last analysis, policies
and actions which are based upon a false or inadequate philosophy can

only lead us into defeat and despair, for even if we hit upon a particular policy which is correct in itself, unless the philosophical basis of our policy is also correct we will make serious mistakes in carrying it through.

We need to understand the world as it really is – which is, broadly speaking, a materialist approach. This approach treats the world as a material force in its own right that exists independently of what we may think it or like it to be. We also need to understand this material world, either in nature or society, as a world of interconnected change and development, a world of universal conflict and contradiction between what is old and dying and what is new and struggling to be born – an approach we call dialectical.

Fused together into a single philosophy, dialectics and materialism enable us to increasingly change the world once we have understood the laws of motion at work in its development. Dialectics alerts us to the need for change, materialism to the importance of bringing this change into line with the objective prevailing circumstances.
There are two basic aspects of Marxist analysis: (1) dialectical materialism, and (2) historical materialism.

Dialectical materialism is a general approach to reality and to our thinking about reality. What does it mean? In everyday speech we often use the word "materialism" to describe the vulgar pursuit of money and material comforts, without any morality or sense of values. This is not what Marxists mean by materialism. Materialism, in the Marxist sense, is an approach that says that we must seek to explain nature, history and society in terms of material realities. Material realities are primary. Ideas are not primary. This kind of materialism is in contrast to philosophical idealism, which argues that ideas are the main explanation for things.

Racism as an Example

Let's take two examples: What are the underlying causes of racism in the U.S.? An idealist might argue that racism is basically the result of racist ideas and attitudes on the part of white Americans. A materialist would say, "Yes, the ideas and attitudes of whites certainly contribute to the racist oppression of African Americans. But how do we explain the origin of these ideas themselves?" The sense of racial superiority by many whites has its roots in material reality – most importantly, racial slavery. These ideas were further consolidated by racial segregation, employment discrimination, and social marginalization. If one thinks that racial oppression is primarily a question of racist ideas, then one would think that the solution is simply the "re-education" of whites, instead of the process of reconstructing the entirety of the political economy of the U.S.

To use another example, an idealist might see the rise of the Tea Party movement as primarily originating as an ideological movement in opposition to an African American president. A materialist would agree on the racist aspect of the Tea Party, but would probe further to understand the material conditions that gave rise to that movement at this particular time in history. While racism certainly motivates the Tea Party, it is primarily an expression of a profound crisis within capitalism, where the current social relations of production (and power) are organized in such a way that they are increasingly incapable of meeting the needs of the people.

Is Materialism Compatible with Religion?

Most progressive religious believers would agree with the points made by our materialist above. However, religious believers would still argue that ultimately a God who is above material realities explains things. For many practical purposes, therefore, there is no argument between progressive believers and nonbelievers. They are all likely to accept a basic materialist approach to history, society and struggle. We know this from our own struggle experience in the Civil Rights Movement, where progressive nonbelievers and believers united in struggle (and united in their materialist analysis of U.S. realities).

However there are forms of religious belief in which God is invoked to explain everything in minute detail. The dollar plunges and we are told that "God is punishing the United States" because there is "too much support for gay equality laws", or for one or another reason. This kind of religious belief clearly does conflict with the attempt to develop a materialist understanding of, for instance, economic realities.

What, then, is dialectics? Marxism argues that material reality must be understood as a dynamic, contradictory and changing process. Moreover, most change is propelled by the internal contradictions of that reality. Marxism has suggested several laws of dialectics which help to illustrate the basically dynamic and contradictory character of real processes.

Quantity into quality: This law reminds us that the increase in the quantity of something can radically change the nature of that reality. A simple physical example is with water. If the temperature of water is steadily raised the water becomes steam, if it is lowered it becomes ice. The change in quantity (in this case the temperature level) can change the quality (or nature) of a thing.

One can also find examples of this law in human society. The Civil Rights Movement of the 1950's set out to protest basic social inequalities in the U.S. As the movement won victories and formal legal equality was attained for African Americans with the passage of the Voting Rights Act (1965), the movement's understanding deepened and it began to question the very nature of how U.S. society is organized, which led to Dr. King's Poor People's Campaign. The Poor People's Campaign led to a qualitative change in the civil rights movement as it began to question the very economic structure of the U.S.

Unity of opposites: The contradictory forces at play in a dialectical process are often not accidental or external to each other. They are often united together in the same process. In a real sense, they often define each other. The one exists because of the other.

The basic law of dialectics can be illustrated by capitalism. The two main opposites in capitalism – the bourgeoisie and the proletariat – exist because of each other. The bourgeoisie came into existence by forcing independent producers (peasants on their own farms) into capitalist controlled factories. But the making of this proletariat was also the making of the bourgeoisie itself. Day-to-day, the bourgeoisie only exists because workers are involved in productive labor in factories, mines, and shops.

Origin of 'White' and Black'

In a social/historical example, "white" Americans (as a concept) came into existence based upon the creation of "black" Americans. As the determination was made (in 1630's Virginia) that "blacks" would be slaves, the determination was also made that "whites" would be free. Thus, the notion of black enslavement is completely bound up with the notion of white freedom. Philosophers make the argument that once you make a determination of the identity of something, you also identify its opposite. Thus, in creating the category of "A", you also create the category of "not A." If there was no "not A," then "A" would have no meaning – as it would be everything. As Hegel said "Every determination is a limitation and every limitation is a determination." By determining something, you limit it and consequently create what it is not.

Negation of the negation: However, the existence of two mutually reproducing realities (for example, the bourgeoisie and the proletariat) does not mean that this has to go on forever. Historically, it was the emerging bourgeoisie that created a proletariat. Now, today, in order to survive as a bourgeoisie, the bourgeoisie needs a proletariat. But the reverse is no longer true. The proletariat can abolish the bourgeoisie and assume control over the economy itself. In this way, the proletariat would end capitalist exploitation and build a society based on social needs, not private profits. This is an example of the "negation of the negation." Capitalism negates the freedom of working people; working people negate the capitalist system of exploitation.

Dialectical materialism is not a foreign ideology. We hope that the examples we have given help to illustrate a key point. There is sometimes a tendency to present dialectical materialism as a complicated and obscure philosophy.

There is also a tendency to present it as the creation of two brilliant European philosophers, Marx and Engels. It is true that Marx and Engels (and other great revolutionaries) helped us to sharpen our tools of analysis, but a basic dialectical and materialist understanding of the world is a common feature of all cultures and societies throughout history.

For instance, there is an old African American proverb that says, "Satan couldn't get along without plenty of help." While premised on the belief of a devil (idealism/religion), it also recognizes that evil in the world is the result of the actions of people (materialism). It is possible to think of hundreds of similar pieces of wisdom from all cultures and people of the world that reflect a dialectical and materialist approach to reality.

One final point must be made about dialectical materialism. We must avoid the idea that dialectical materialism is some magic formula that provides all the answers. It is not "truth eyeglasses" – put them on and you can understand everything! (To think like this that would be to fall, precisely, into idealism! No set of ideas, including dialectical materialism, has all the answers ready made.) Dialectical materialism provides us with some general ways of approaching reality. It reminds us that reality is complex, contradictory, and changing.

Put another way, dialectical materialism reminds us that our ideas (including our Marxist ideas) are always at best, approximations to the truth. Reality is likely always to surprise us a bit. Our job is to constantly discuss, debate, build on our collective understanding and try out our ideas, strategies and policies in practice. We must inform our practice, our collective struggle, with ideas. But we must also continually assess what our practice has taught us. No theory, including Marxism, is written in stone. Marxism is itself a dynamic, evolving and living theory. In our own struggles, debates, and policy formulation we are contributing to that evolution.

Historical Materialism

Dialectical materialism is a general philosophical approach to reality. Historical materialism is the more specific study of societies and of human history. It is based on the understanding that our history is the history of classes and of class struggle.

The most basic idea of Marxism is that societies must be understood from a class perspective. Economic policy, or the kind of democracy that exists, or how schooling is organized – all of these things, and many more, must be assessed from a class perspective. A policy that is good for the bourgeoisie is not necessarily good for working people.
But what are classes? In general discussion we often refer loosely to the poor and the rich, to middle classes, and so on. The fact that there are poor people and rich people is an indication of the existence of classes, but for Marxism it is important to develop a more precise understanding of what we mean by classes.

Classes are the result of the ways in which production is organized in societies. All forms of production involve two basic things. Forces of production: these are the basic requirements of production; tools, machines, transport, land, raw materials, capital, labor, etc. and Relations of production: this refers to how people come together (as owners, workers, managers) in the process of production. These two combine to form the mode of production.

Modes of Production

In the course of history there have been several different ways in which production has been organized. These different ways of organizing production are referred to as modes of production. Capitalism and socialism are, for instance, two different modes of production. Among the major modes of production in history are:

Early communist or communal societies. All human societies seem to have evolved from small bands of people involved in basic hunting of game, and gathering of vegetation. At this stage people were nomadic – they moved around following wild game. However, some people began to develop their forces of production. Wild animals were tamed and bred. Societies began herding sheep, goats and cattle. In addition to these activities, societies also began to cultivate crops – like rice. Now they could be more settled, because most of their food could be found in one place.
All human societies – in Europe, Africa, Australia, Asia and the Americas – followed this path of development. There was a lot of equality in these societies. There was no such thing as rulers or exploited people. Everyone who was old enough, and healthy enough, worked in the fields or hunted or herded, or built houses and tools. People shared the work. There was no such thing as unemployment. Everyone's contribution was valuable. In times of plenty, everyone ate well. In times of shortage, everyone went hungry. There were, sometimes, small social inequalities

between young and old, or between men and women – but they were not remotely like the huge inequalities between rich and poor, privileged and marginalized, in modern capitalist societies. These early classless societies existed for thousands of years, and many survived into modern times.

So how and why did class societies emerge? We're not sure exactly how the earliest class societies emerged. This probably happened in many different ways, in different places. What is clear is that the development of the forces of production (with the rearing of herds and the cultivation of crops), created the conditions in which property could be accumulated (stored). This meant that some groups could become much richer than others. They could even use these powers to raid, dispossess, and oppress other groups.

As a result of this kind of process, class societies began to develop. One of the earliest forms of class society was slavery. The slave mode of production involved two basic classes – the slave owners and the slaves. The slave owners owned all of the forces of production (including the slaves themselves), while the slaves did all of the work. Slaves were basically prisoners of the masters.

From the Bible we know that there were powerful slave societies in ancient times – like the Egypt of the pharaohs in which a whole people, the Israelites, were the slaves and treated as beasts of burden. The lives of most of the slaves were very hard. Most were treated as prisoners. They were kept at night in tiny cells. Many had no family life. Children could be bought or sold to different slave masters. Whipping and other brutal punishments were common when recaptured, slaves who ran away were flogged, branded with a red-hot iron and sentenced to a lifetime in chains. A second attempt to run away could result in the slave having ears, the tip of the nose, and sometimes the right hand cut off. Runaways were frequently hanged.

This is not to say that slaves did not fight against their oppressors. There were many slave revolts in ancient history – Spartacus led one of the most famous in first century B.C. Rome. There was another large revolt of African slaves in what is now Iraq in the ninth century, involving nearly half a million slaves. However, the conditions under which slaves were kept made organization and unity very difficult. These heroic revolts were typically crushed with great brutality.

It's also important to remember that there are differences between ancient slavery (as in Biblical or Roman days) and modern slavery in the U.S., Latin America, and the Caribbean. There are many similarities, but the key difference is that modern slavery developed as a key element of the capitalist mode of production. These modern day slaves were totally integrated into a developing world capitalist economy as the products of their labor (sugar, cotton, and rice) were the commodities that built the international economy.

Feudalism and Land

Feudalism was another early form of class society. Like slavery, feudalism was found in many parts of the world. In feudalism there are also two main classes – those who either owned or controlled the land (the feudal lords) and those who did the work (the serfs). Unlike slaves, however, who owned nothing, the serfs were small farmers, or peasants. They worked on a little bit of land, and owned some of the tools – maybe a cart, an ox, a spade, and a plow.

Under this system, the feudal lord forced the serfs to give up some of their own products, like crops or milk, that they had produced on the land. For instance, they might have to give one out of every four bags of corn. They were also often forced to work for part of the year, without any payment, on the feudal lords lands.

Feudalism was a kind of robbery or forced taxation. The feudal lords took from the serf (without payment) produce and labor. Although the system did not develop very strongly in most of Africa or the Americas, it is clear that many tribal societies were beginning to move from early communalism toward some kind of feudalism controlled by traditional leaders.

One important fact about both slavery and feudalism was that they were usually quite backward in the machinery they used for production. Slave owners made fortunes by treating their slaves as animals who could be forced to do nothing but hard, manual work. Feudalism was fairly similar. The machinery used was usually the basic tool owned by poor peasants. But developing slowly in the corners of these earlier class societies was a revolutionary new system of production, which would change the face of the world – capitalism.

Like slavery and feudalism, capitalism involves two main classes – one exploiting the other. In capitalism it is the bourgeoisie that exploits the working class (or proletariat). As with slavery, today's workers do not own the main means of production – factories, mines, machinery, banks, and shops. Those are owned and controlled by the bourgeoisie. However, unlike slavery, in capitalism, the exploited workers are not sold themselves. What is sold is their labor power; they sell their labor power on the labor market in exchange for a wage. Modern workers are not typically held prisoners by the bosses, like slaves were. Of course, modern workers are not really "free." In fact, hunger, mass unemployment, debt, and the need to earn money to survive forces workers "voluntarily" into the system of capitalism.

Unlike under feudalism where the serfs worked for the lords and with their own tools, under capitalism, workers work in their hundreds and thousands in factories, farms, mines, shops and banks. From an organizational point of view, this much more advanced form of production organization is crucial. Capitalism brings together many thousands of workers in the production process, and, in this way, capitalism itself begins to organize workers. As Marx and Engels said, "The bourgeoisie gives birth to its own grave digger."

The basis of capitalist class exploitation lies in the difference between the daily wage paid to the worker and the new value that the worker produces in the course of working each day.

The first capitalists had small factories, more like small workshops. They employed about ten workers. These workshops produced goods like shoes. Each small capitalist would pay the ten workers enough for them to buy food and clothes for themselves and their families. Let us say it was one dollar a day for each worker. But at the same time the worker was producing about two dollars worth of goods for the boss to sell. This means the boss was getting one dollars worth of work free from each worker each day.

If the boss was employing ten workers this means he was making ten dollars extra every day. With this, of course, the boss still had to buy the raw material to make the goods. He had to pay for the maintenance of the workshop and the machines. Let us say that once he has done this, he has made five dollars profit for the day.

This was the secret of capitalism. What we have described is a very small capitalist workshop at the beginnings of capitalism. But the same secret of creating profit from the work of others remains as the basis of today's capitalism.

All the small-time capitalists dreamed of bigger things. Why employ only ten workers and get only five dollars profit a day? Why not employ 100 or 1,000 workers and make $100 our $1,000 a day for yourself? In this simple question lies a tendency for capitalism to involve greater concentrations of production. Why get only two dollars worth of new value from each worker every day? Why not push workers harder, make them work longer hours, or at greater speed? In these questions, which every capitalist still asks every day, we see the secret of the capitalist pursuit of greater intensity of work, of more machinery, of greater productivity, and thus, greater profit.

Why pay workers one dollar a day if you can force them to work for less? Herein lies the ongoing tendency for capitalism to exploit unemployment, poverty and desperation to force workers to work harder for less. It is also what underpins globalization – the pursuit of cheaper labor power in distant parts of the world.

Maybe you don't need to increase the misery of workers to make wages less. Maybe with machinery you can produce cheaper clothing, cheaper food, and therefore you can also lower your wage bill because the cost of living for your workers will decline. Herein lies a tendency for capitalism to constantly seek to revolutionize the forces of production through technical innovation.

This brief description of how capitalism tends to work will be familiar to any worker on the shop floor. The profit-seeking nature of capitalism makes them both a highly revolutionary, highly dynamic mode of production, and also a deeply exploitative system.

Not Just Two Classes

Capitalism is rooted in exploitation in production. This exploitation in production is based on two main classes – the bourgeoisie and the workers. However, in any society, including in modern capitalist societies, there are usually other classes and social strata. A class approach to capitalism means that we seek to understand the main dynamic of capitalism in terms of the contradiction and struggle between capitalists and workers. But this does not mean that we can reduce everything to this contradiction. The existence of other classes and social strata within the two main classes are an important phenomenon.

Before we discuss these issues, let's step back and develop a more rigorous definition and analysis of class. The accepted Marxist definition of classes is "... large groups of people differing from each other by the place they occupy in a historically determined system of production, by their relation (in most cases fixed and formulated in law) to the means of production, by their role in the social organization of labor, and, consequently, by the dimensions of the share of social wealth of which they dispose in the mode of acquiring it."
Of these four class-forming criteria, Lenin singled out two as being primary. He stated that, "The fundamental criteria by which classes are distinguished is the place they occupy in social production, and, consequently, the relation in which they stand to the means of production."

Thus, these four class-forming criteria do not have equal weight. The first criterion – the place occupied in a historically determined system of production – aims at viewing groups of people according to where they stand in relation to the production and appropriation of surplus value, as producers of surplus value or extractors of surplus value from others. Consequently, this criterion is aimed at the very logic of the capitalist system, the production of surplus value. In a society based upon exploitation, as capitalism is, this must be part of the fundamental criterion, as Lenin has suggested.

Where one stands in relation to the second criterion – relationship to the means of production – is largely determined by the first criterion, that is, if one exists through the exploitation of workers, one probably owns the means of production. On the other hand, if one produces surplus value, then one is likely to be divorced from the means of production. However, there are many workers in developed capitalist society who don't produce surplus value, such as teachers, social workers, and public service workers – more about this later.

The third criterion – role in the social organization of labor – concerns issues such as decision-making and management.

Finally, the fourth criterion – share of the social wealth – is primarily concerned with income and wealth.

Thus, Marxism takes a dialectical view of class, attempting to view it in an all-sided manner. This is in contrast to bourgeois theories, which take a relatively narrow view by focusing primarily on income.

Productive and Unproductive Labor

When looked at from this view, workers such as public service workers (teachers, firemen, social workers, etc.) are part of the working class. They perform labor, but it is non-productive labor. Categorizing their labor as "non-productive" is not a value judgment. It simply means they don't produce surplus value. They don't produce surplus value because their labor is exchanged for public revenue, not capital. In Theories of Surplus Values, Marx makes very clear that the concrete type of labor has nothing to do with the production of surplus value. He uses the example of a juggler. If the juggler stands on a corner and makes his money from the contributions of pedestrians, he is not creating surplus value since his labor is being exchanged for personal revenue. If, however, that juggler works for a circus, he is producing surplus value, since his labor is being exchanged for private capital. Consequently, it's the social relationship in which the labor is exchanged that creates the production of surplus value.

On the other hand, a professional baseball player may earn ten million dollars per year. He doesn't own the means of production and he works in a capitalist enterprise and exchanges his labor for capital. He produces surplus value, but is he a worker? Based on his share of the social wealth, he is not a worker and would be more likely to share the same lifestyle and broad social outlook as a typical capitalist. Consequently, we can't simply look at what a person does for a living, or how much money they make to determine their class position in society.

Classes themselves are not homogenous. Within the bourgeoisie there are various sub-classes, for example there are the monopoly bourgeoisie, the middle bourgeoisie, and the petit-bourgeoisie. They are mostly stratified by the amount of capital they control and consequently their role in the economy. The monopoly bourgeoisie are increasingly globally based. They are the smallest sector (in numbers) of the bourgeoisie, but the most powerful. The middle bourgeoisie are large business owners, but are mostly based within the U.S. Finally, the petit-bourgeoisie are the largest sector in number, but the smallest in the amount of capital they control. They range from owners of small businesses with one or several workers to mid-range businesses with several hundred workers. This includes professionals who may be self-employed as lawyers, physicians, etc. although these professions are becoming increasingly proletarianized.

Although all of the above categories are all members of the bourgeoisie, their differing status means that they don't necessarily have the same class interests at all times. For example, the monopoly bourgeoisie may favor bank bailouts for the wealthiest banks, while the petit-bourgeoisie may not see that as being in their interest. In many cases, the petit-bourgeoisie may even align with the workers.

The working class is also stratified. Within the working class there are industrial workers, service workers, public employees, etc. – some of whom produce surplus value and some of whom don't. While, in general and objectively, they share the same class interests they may see specific issues differently. For example, a private, non-unionized worker may resent the fact that a unionized public worker, doing the same job, has better wages and pensions. Although the reason the public worker has better pay and benefits is because he/she is unionized, the non-union, private worker, who pays the taxes that fund the public worker, may be susceptible to right-wing propaganda about "overpaid" public workers.

Another increasing strata of the working class are the long-term unemployed. This is a problem that is particularly located in the urban, and nationally oppressed communities. Their interests also coincide with the employed workers, but a section of them, due to their proximity to lumpen, or the criminal, element have the potential to become disruptive elements in working class communities.

In addition to classes and strata, capitalist society is also segmented in a number of significant areas. Some of the key areas in the U.S. are the segments of nationality and gender. We looked at the basic economic exploitation at the heart of capitalism. However capitalist societies also use and intensify a range of other social mechanics to maintain bourgeois rule. This includes gender, race and ideological oppression.

The use of ethnic prejudices (national chauvinism) has long been a tool used by the bourgeoisie to divide the working class. Here it is useful to make a demarcation between what is commonly referred to as "racism" and "national oppression." Racism, when used colloquially, is often employed to describe all forms of national oppression.

Racism vs. National Oppression

However, for a more scientific analysis it is useful to distinguish between racism, as a form of ideology, and national oppression, which is a historically rooted, material manifestation of oppression. Further, since there is no scientific definition of race, what we call "racism" in the realm of ideology is more properly termed "chauvinism." Thus, when we use the term national oppression, we are referring to what some might call "institutional racism" and when we use the term national chauvinism we are referring to what is popularly termed "racism."

The bourgeoisie to maintain and legitimize national oppression manipulates chauvinism. For example, if all chauvinist ideas magically disappeared from society today, African Americans would still suffer from disproportionate unemployment, poor educational facilities, substandard housing, etc. In fact, chauvinist attitudes have gone through a remarkable change in the past fifty years, while the social conditions of African Americans have deteriorated. Alleviating these conditions would be possible, but it would take a tremendous amount of government revenue and political will to bring about these changes. One of the central reasons for the lack of this political will are the chauvinist-based notions that African Americans are in there present condition because they have no desire to improve their situation – they are lazy, only want government handouts, etc.

Of course African Americans aren't the only nationally oppressed people in the U.S., but the African American question is central due to the history of their experience in the U.S.

Social divisions rooted in gender differences are often used in a capitalist economy to protect the level of profitability and to create divisions among the working class. Patriarchy refers to male domination in all spheres of society, including the economy, the household, the state, the law, schools and religion. Patriarchy takes different forms in different societies, and affects women from different classes and national groups differently.

Three important ways in which gender and national divisions help to ensure profitability include the performance of unpaid labor, discrimination, and segmentation.

Unpaid Labor

The advent of capitalism and its interrelationship with patriarchal domination resulted in the intensification of the household sexual division of labor and the marginalization of women in wage work. The sexual division of labor refers to a situation where men and women perform different kinds of work. There is evidence that the sexual division of labor existed before the advent of capitalism in most countries and capital adopted and utilized divisions such as gender and nationality to its own advantage. In pre-capitalist society there was no geographical separation between different forms of work, which made the impact of the sexual division of labor less severe, and women played a significant role in production. The development of industrial capitalism resulted in an increase in commodity production outside of the household, and the separation of the household from the waged workplace. Men entered into wage work away from the household, while women came to be regarded exclusively as housewives, and the work they did was not seen as wage labor. The physical location of production therefore shifted away from the household, with capital making no provision for childbearing or rearing, this being regarded as undesired costs.

This situation meant that women experienced difficulties in combining ways to work with childcare and domestic work, resulting in an intensification of the sexual division of labor. Childcare became an increased responsibility for women, as it could no longer be easily incorporated with their economic activities.

Domestic ideology developed along with the separation of the household from the wage workplace to reinforce women's household role. Women and men are regarded differently, with women seen primarily as domestic workers, and expected to give priority to this work over wage work. This division of labor and the associated domestic ideology greatly increases women's economic dependence on men, and their subordinate position in the household.

The surplus produced in a capitalist economy is protected by a substantial amount of unpaid labor performed primarily by women. A substantial amount of labor is performed in households in any economy. Services such as preparing meals, maintaining the home, raising and educating children, and caring for the sick, disabled, and elderly require a substantial amount of labor time. Much of this labor is unpaid and even when it is paid (e.g. domestic service workers) it is undervalued. This unpaid household labor is often called reproductive labor, because it is necessary for households (both worker and capitalist) to reproduce themselves. Without someone working to raise children, for example, the next generation of workers would not be available to keep the economy going. Therefore, a capitalist economy depends critically on the substantial amount of non-capitalists unpaid labor.

Discrimination

Discrimination in terms of wages received – in which men and whites receive higher wages than do women and nationally oppressed people – can be used to protect profitability. The availability of cheap labor means that profits can be maintained and increased by using more highly exploited workers. Women are often employed in low-wage industries, for example, textile manufacturing, as a way of protecting the surplus produced.

Labor Segmentation. Segmentation is a broad term and it refers to people being separated into different industries, different types of jobs in different levels of skill and responsibility. Patriarchal ideology influences definitions of skill, with wage work carried out by women almost always regarded as less skilled and less valuable. It also influences the type of work that women and men do, with women mostly doing carrying or cleaning work (similar to the work they do in the household). Women tend to be nurses while men tend to be doctors. Women tend to be clerical workers while men tend to be managers. Because the work that women do is undervalued, they are often segmented into relatively lower paying and lower status jobs. The same applies to national classifications. Whites tend to be segmented into higher skilled, more "professional," and higher paid jobs, while people belonging to oppressed nationalities are segmented into lower paid, unskilled employment.

Segmentation supports the capitalist drive for profitability by creating divisions among workers. Such divisions make collective action on the part of workers more difficult and weaken the overall power of labor. Categories of nationality and gender are socially constructed – they are inventions of society – which have become incorporated into the functioning of the economy. While these categories are simply social inventions, they have dramatic real consequences – high levels of poverty and deprivation among women, children and the nationally oppressed. Both these characteristics – the artificial nature of the divisions and their real historic and current consequences – must be kept in mind when analyzing nationality and gender dynamics within a capitalist economy.

Finally nationality and gender divisions are often conflated with class divisions. For example, white men dominate the capitalist class and women perform the majority of the unpaid labor in society. It should be stressed, however, the class divisions are not the same as nationality and gender divisions. White workers can be chauvinists in order to protect their privileged position and labor unions can maintain a high level of sexism within the rank-and-file.

Does it make any difference what a person's class or strata is? Marxists generally believe that a person's social condition plays a significant role in the formation of their thought and in their political and social beliefs and that a society's mode of production broadly reflects the ideological currents in that society. Marxists often paraphrase Marx by noting that, "Social being determines social consciousness."

How then do we untangle the economic forces from the social/ideological/political forces in society?

In his *Preface to A Contribution to the Critique of Political Economy,* Marx wrote, "In the social production of their existence, men inevitably enter into definite relations, which are independent of their will, namely relations of production appropriate to a given stage in the development of their material forces of production. The totality of these relations of production constitutes the economic structure of society, the real foundation, on which arises a legal and political superstructure and to which correspond definite forms of social consciousness. The mode of production of material life conditions the general process of social, political and intellectual life."

The above passage, often misunderstood by those influenced by Marx, contains a possible key to unraveling the connection between ideology and economics. Marx clearly states that the mode of production of material life (we'll call that 'economics' for the moment) conditions the ideological structure of society. This is far from positing that economics determines ideology. Many historians who have been influenced by Marx have misunderstood this simple passage and have often substituted a crude form of economic determinism for a genuinely, complex historical-materialist analysis. What is meaningful in Marx's statement is that while ideology arises from the economic foundation, it is merely conditioned by that foundation – and after it has arisen it develops in reaction to changes in economic life as well as possessing an internal life and logic of its own. Thus, ideological changes are not just a simple, direct reflection of economic changes in society. Rather changes in the mode of production are translated into and through ideological changes, which themselves change and develop within the context of their own logic.

Marx's statement following the one quoted above potentially leads to further confusion. He wrote, "It is not the consciousness of men that determines their existence, but their social existence that determines their consciousness." Here, we finally encounter the dreaded "d" word. However, the word "determines" in this context is best understood in its literal meaning that is from the Latin determinare, or "to limit or set boundaries." Consequently, the mode of production simply sets boundaries – or limits – the area within which consciousness operates. It doesn't strictly define or determine consciousness.

Production Relations Are Between People

Finally, one must keep in mind that the mode of production consists of the forces of production and the relations of production within any society. The relations of production are relations between people, who carry within them all of the ideological constructs that arise from their interaction with others – especially, but not solely, in the process of material production. Thus, it is theoretically incorrect to pose the "economy" against "ideology," for the way the term "economy" is used actually includes the ideological realm as it is manifested within the relations of production, i.e., relations between people.

Why then do people often oppose their own class interest? For the answer to that question we must examine the role of ideology in society. Ideology. Under capitalism the ideas of the capitalist class are everywhere – in schools, in newspapers, on television and film, and advertisements, even in churches and religious institutions. These ideas convey a simple and clear message – that the capitalist system is good, that it is natural and inevitable. Inequality is not seen as part of the system, or as something that is caused by the system. Instead it is seen as a result of individual differences. The advertisements that we see every day and the messages that we get through films and other media is that anyone who works hard enough can make it in the capitalist system.

These ideas also introduce materialistic values. People are made to think that if you have lots of things you are powerful and respectable. Capitalism, particularly the advertising industry, makes people think that they need things that they actually do not need at all. This is what we call consumerism – the urge to constantly buy more and more material things, and the belief that these things will bring happiness and fulfillment. Capitalism also tells us that we cannot rely on other people. That everyone is naturally greedy and corrupt, and that we live in the world of "each to his own" and "dog eats dog," and that this is the natural order of things.

The key elements of capitalist ideology promote consumerism, individualism and passivity in the acceptance of all forms of oppression. This ideology disguises oppression, or blames it on the groups that are oppressed.

If these groups hear the message often enough, they too begin to believe it. We call this internalized oppression. For example, working-class people are made to feel that they cannot think, that they are not intelligent, and that their only value is the work they do. Women are made to think their only use is to make a man happy and look after children. The society judges and values people by the work that they do, and people are given an inferior or superior status on that basis.

Under the capitalist system workers are forced to sell their labor – they have to choose between working for the capitalists or destitution. Workers are caught in a vicious cycle in which their labor makes the rich richer and at the same time makes the society more consumerist and money oriented. They become cogs in the system.

What is ideology? Theory generally refers to a set of ideas, while ideology refers to the relationship between ideas and society or a particular social class. Marx argued that ideas are really rooted in reality. Ideas influence society and society influences ideas – this is a two-way process (a dialectic).

Theory is not neutral – it is based on power relations in class society. Ideas are strongly influenced by the way in which society is organized, how we get food and shelter, how we produce and distribute goods, the material "mode of production." This means that our thinking and ideas do not exist in a vacuum but are strongly influenced by our class, race, gender, and other social positions and experiences. Marx argued, "The ideas of the ruling class are in every epoch the ruling ideas." He argued that the ruling class controls the means of material production, but also controls intellectual production.

Ideology is what blinds workers to the injustice of exploitation. Marx refers to this as "false consciousness," referring to the acceptance of the ideology of the ruling class, while believing that it is your own individual thought or belief. Organizations that mobilize the working class aim to challenge the ideas that support injustice, and to create a new set of ideas (ideology) for liberation. Thus, capitalist ideology can make workers passive, and willing to accept their oppressions, but revolutionary ideology prepares workers for struggle to change society.

Questions for Discussion

1. What are some examples of people relying upon idealism instead of a materialist analysis?

2. How has racism been used to divide the working class and derail the struggle for democracy?

3. What sector, if any, of the working class is it more important to organize politically?

4. What are some examples of workers' false consciousness?

The Strategy of Attrition

This article, treating the topic of strategy and the state as they apply to both revolutionary and mass organization, recently appeared of the web site, The North Star, January 1, 2014, http://www.thenorthstar.info/ Reprinted here with permission from the authors.

Part One: Conquest or Destruction of the State?

By Gavin Mendel-Gleason & James O'Brien

Introduction

Right from its beginnings in early 19th century, socialism has been bedeviled by debates over strategy in a way that right-wing ideologies have not. Would salvation come, as Fourier dreamed, from wealthy benefactors funding new communist colonies or maybe, as Proudhon envisaged, through workers founding their own mutualist enterprises and bypassing politics altogether?

Or perhaps a more aggressive stance was necessary, as advocated by the proto-syndicalist wing of the British Chartist movement in the 1830s, who even then were cognizant of workers' leverage at the point of production and supported the use of a Grand National Holiday — aka a general strike. Or was the mainstream Chartist emphasis on political action, i.e. taking control of state-power after having won universal suffrage, the best way forward.

These strands and more were already manifest in England, then the most advanced capitalist country, in the 1830s — a long time ago. And they remain with us to this day because the problem to which they attempted to solve, namely minority rule, remains very much with us. The various tendencies correspond to available oppositional niches in a society dominated by capitalist production and therefore elite influence.

It seems obvious that an adroit mixture of the strategies, one which combined the strength of labor, the potential wealth of co-ops and the leverage of mass parties, is the goldilocks of political strategies and indeed that is the position we advocate. However, once we get into the details the obvious quickly becomes very blurry indeed. It's hardly surprising that socialists have lacked the clarity of the right-wing since they, unlike us, are in driving seat and don't need to change a whole lot while we are searching for a way to achieve our goals.

And it turns out that a combined arms strategy of unions, co-ops, and political party is not, in fact, the dominant orientation on the radical left, and has not been since 1917, at least in the English speaking world. There are, for example, proponents of an exclusively non-state orientation and there are supporters of political means, but who both deny that co-operatives can play a meaningful role before the working class has seized power and that tightly knit revolutionary groups are the key to success.

In this essay we are going to focus on the political arena and make case for a robust mass party strategy that aims to win political power via democratic elections, and only touch upon the role of trade unions and co-ops.

The Democratic Road

The case for choosing the democratic road is best teased out in comparison with alternative approaches, which for our purposes is going to mostly be the strategy of insurrection pursued by Anarchists and Trotskyists that is common amongst the revolutionary groups in the Anglo-phone world.

If the basic strategic choices first emerged in the 1830s, they became permanent features of the political landscape in the era of the First International (1864 – 1873) when the Anarchists and the Marxists parted ways replete with their own theoretical justifications. The Russian Revolutions of 1905 and 1917, which saw the emergence of workers' councils, moved the debate from being one that separated Anarchists and Marxists and landed it into the heart of Marxism itself.

Let us lay our cards on the table at the outset: the political strategy advocated here involves attempting to win state power in the advanced capitalist countries through legal means, taking the democratic road if you will. In practice, this involves winning a majority through competition in elections which are broadly considered free and fair.

However, a simple description of this approach isn't sufficient. In order to evaluate its worth, we need to compare it to alternatives, of which there is no shortage, from anti-consumerism, to back to nature primitivism, NGO lobbying, Third Worldism, and Occupyesque protesting to name some of the lesser lights. For reasons of space, we're going to limit the alternative to the principal one offered by revolutionary socialists since 1917: the smashing of the existing state and its replacement by participatory workers councils, i.e. the primary strategy offered by both the Trotskyists and the Anarchists. Moreover, we need a way of choosing between the alternatives. As the debate between them has gone on since the days of the First International, it seems likely that both sides have valid points to make. For instance, James Bierly, in a recent article on the North Star catalogued the many practical advantages of electoralism, such as the opportunities to engage with regular people that simply aren't there when you are hawking the Socialist Worker at a demonstration. On the other hand, the anti-parliamentary left highlights the limitations of parliament in being able to bring capital under control given the strength of the unelected bureaucracy.

Hard Decisions

The problem with these arguments is not that they are not true. Quite the opposite: the problem is that they are true, i.e. both the pro and anti parliamentary strategies have valid arguments for their respective points of view. This makes it hard to decide in favour of one or the other strategy.

The pro and anti-electoral arguments pass each other like ships in the night because they are embedded in different theoretical frameworks. The anti-electoralist position of the Anarchists, for example, is not a stand alone affair but one that follows ineluctably from their opposition to hierarchies and representation. Similarly, the Leninist view that the positive use of electoralism is confined to more or less propaganda opportunities is derived from their view of the state as a capitalist entity which cannot be wielded by the working class for their own liberation. Rather it must be smashed and, as with the Anarchists, replaced with a form more appropriate to workers' self-emancipation. [Note: in this essay, rather than constantly write "the Anarchists and the Leninists", we're going to describe their common position of smashing the state as "insurrectionary" or, more rarely, as "revolutionary".]

So, the question as to whether socialists should put effort into running for elections and, if so, how much, can't just be answered by listing the positive aspects of participating in elections because that case doesn't address the issue of the state form being inherently capitalist, nor the issue of representation giving rise to oppressive hierarchies. The revolutionary opponents, or at least the more thoughtful elements, of the strategy already know those positive aspects. It's just that in their framework these factors are outweighed by the counter-tendencies. Such a list serves a useful function in confirming the faith of the already converted, but does little to expand the coterie of modern day centrists.

Now, it isn't possible to exhaustively deal with all the points, even in a fairly lengthy article like this one. Rather, we want to make explicit the theoretical framework in which electoralism is embedded. It is the entirety of the strategy that needs to be weighed against the entirety of the insurrectionary approach, not just electoralism per se, although that is our focus here. First let's turn to the underlying logic of the anti-parliamentary left.

Revolution and the State

This need to smash the state, which is the core strategic aim of so many radical left groups, chimes with the language of the 19th century socialist movement, from which the modern insurrectionary groups are descended. There were no shortage of revolutions from the period 1789 to 1936 in Europe and the concept became very firmly embedded in their DNA.

But revolution can mean different things: e.g. it's sometimes used in general way to describe deep change in the social structure, e.g. the women's revolution or industrial revolution both of which involved a decades long project.

Then there is the concept of revolution as a new class coming to power, such as the rise to dominance of the bourgeoisie in France through the revolutionary 1790s. But a transfer of class power can occur in a lot of different ways, e.g. in France in the Great Revolution it was sudden and bloody, but in many countries, like Sweden or Denmark, the bourgeoise came to power peacefully and gradually. And it's worth remembering that countries like Sweden were aristocracies from which the bourgeoisie were excluded from exercising state power and that it took decades of struggle before they were given the keys to government.

There is also a more directly political but nonetheless metaphorical use of the term, as when Mélenchon, one of the leaders of the the Left Front in France, issues a ringing call for a citizen's revolution or when Syriza's Tspiras likewise calls for 'peaceful revolution'. In this case, while they are looking to greatly extend democracy and engage in structural reform of the state apparatus, they are not calling for it to be smashed and replaced with new organs of democracy.

And it is this ruptural meaning of revolution as an extra-legal seizure of power, not necessarily by coup d'état, but by perhaps by street demonstrations such as we saw in Eastern Europe in 1989 or in St Petersburg in 1917, and the destruction of the administrative apparatus that gives rise to a hostility to socialist electoralism. Attempting to win power, let alone win power democratically, to an entity you intend to abolish is clearly not going to be a high priority.

The attractiveness of conquering or destroying state power depends on our conception of the state. For those firmly situated in the Anarchist or Leninist traditions, the modern state is a capitalist one and cannot, therefore, be wielded by the working class for their own liberation. Instead it must be smashed and new, participatory organs put in its place. The reasoning underlying the need to smash it is that the state is ultimately the guarantor of capitalist domination and capitalists aren't likely to be too accommodating in giving up their control of investment simply because a socialist party attains a majority. The putsch in Chile in 1973 is the favourite example of what the right-wing will resort to if their control of property is called into question, but there are no shortage of others: Spain 1936 is another big one. Indeed, European fascism is hard to understand without an appreciation of the fear that the elites had of a growing socialist-labor movement taking power democratically. Moreover, for the insurrectionaries, democracy in the advanced capitalist countries is a sham, with the resources available to the pro-capitalist media and politicians ensuring that the right-wing are always strong enough to win enough support to prevent the socialists from implementing their program.

Thus, destruction of the state is the order of the day, with the point of note being the sequence: first, the state, as the godfather of capital, must be taken out of the equation; only then can the working class organize, through new forms such as workers' councils, the mass participation in public life necessary to the complete the journey to socialism. In the absence of its protector, capital itself is vulnerable to expropriation by the masses, and so the revolution can move in a radical direction very quickly.

Like all good theories it carries with it some clear implications for current political activity in that the form of organizations that we aim to build are designed with the insurrectionary scenario in mind. Until a revolutionary situation arises in which the state can be smashed there are limits to what can be achieved on a mass scale since it is the process of revolution itself that draws the masses into public life.1 When revolution finally does break out, the new organs of democracy, the councils, will be the vehicle of mass participation.

The consequences for a socialist electoralism follows the chain of logic: since the state is capitalist, it cannot be a vehicle for socialist transformation and since it's is not a vehicle for socialist transformation, elections to gain power is a nonsensical strategy. And since insurrectionary socialists have no interest in winning state power via elections, they have no need to construct political organizations that are capable of doing so. Instead, they seek to create political organizations suited to their fundamental theoretical understanding of what socialist transformation should look like, i.e. mass participatory councils with a revolutionary party as an aide.

The political position in favor of a revolutionary party coupled with mass assemblies is dual organizationalist. The compliment of mass councils is the need for an explicitly revolutionary party that interacts with the masses during the revolutionary process and is the repository of the historical mission in less propitious times. But the revolutionary party itself has a different role than the workers councils and remains separate from them and pre-revolutionary mass organizations. By separate we mean institutionally distinct, not that they never try to influence them. Although naturally a pro-insurrectionary party would like to grow, it doesn't aim to win a majority support for itself, as an organization, but instead view the emergence of councils as the entrance of the masses onto the stage of history.

That, in summary form, is what we'd call the classic view of the primacy of insurrection, one that was described as 'strategy of overthrow' in the debates of the early 20th Century and subsequently became dominant in the Anglo-sphere far left, primarily through the proliferation of Trotskyist parties, but also in substantially the same, if less irritating, form of class struggle Anarchist groups.

The Capitalist State

If an insurrectionary political strategy rests upon the state as an inherently capitalist force, then it also falls if the state doesn't match that premise. The record of the state protecting private property in the means of production has provoked a long-running debate within Marxism about the relationship between the state and capitalism, with views ranging from seeing it as a good old fashioned executive committee of the bourgeoisie to emphasizing its relative autonomy from the capitalist class.

At the more simple end of the spectrum, then, Marxists see the state as a form of class rule. It is not a free floating entity above the messy reality of class conflict but rather a tool for suppressing the exploited, that is, an organizational tool of those in control of the means of production. For much of history, this is essentially an accurate description and it remains fundamentally true to this day. In Ireland alone, the continuous and truly massive transfer of wealth from workers to capitalists arising from the latter's losses in property speculation is a graphic illustration of the balance of class power. There is no question of a transfer of wealth in the other direction.

But modern society is more complicated than pre-capitalist social formations. The exploited are not as powerless and thus have gained a measure of influence over the state itself, the degree of which depends on the balance of class forces at any given juncture. The strength of the working class in Europe over the 20th century is reflected in the significant gains that it made, winning concessions on everything from maternity pay to lower retirement, from national health services to a reduction in militarism.

The western state is open to influence by other sectors. That is, it is dominated by capitalists and will, when push comes to shove, tend to favour their interests rather than those of other sectors. That tendency, however, demonstrates not that the state is intrinsically structured to deliver capitalism but that the social dominance of the capitalists manifests itself in the political choices made by those who control the state. Capitalist control of the investment process is key because most states are dependent on capitalists for a functioning economy, which itself is necessary to keep its population relatively satisfied and to generate income via taxation.

Balance of Power is Critical

The state's own capacity to reproduce itself, then, is dependent on capitalist investment but importantly it is not itself a capitalist formation as is proven by the existence of non-capitalist sovereign powers throughout history. The state, as a powerful entity with a distinct history and a degree of freedom regarding accruing resources, could attempt to usurp the capitalist position by supplanting its role in the investment process. Indeed, that is what we largely advocate. But the current configuration of power within the state apparatus more or less accurately reflects capitalist power in society at large and a process of democratization of the state is best seen as a parallel process to democratizing the ownership of capital itself, rather than as either as a precursor or a successor to it. Until that balance of power is altered there is little reason to expect the state to escape its subservience to the needs of capitalists.

The state, in other words, does not operate on capitalist lines. It operates in a capitalist context. The mode of production is king not because every activity becomes capitalist (or feudal or whatever) — a position which would see it expand like a rogue Agent Smith in the Matrix films and become everything and therefore lose all explanatory power — but because it exerts the decisive selective pressure on all other social forms, including the state itself. If any social group wishes to prosper it needs to bring its behavior into line with the dominant mode of production. Thus, non-capitalist groups, such as amateur sports clubs, often go cap in hand to capitalist corporations for sponsorship while many scientific researchers depend on them for funding.[2] Because capitalism remains the strongest method of producing, those states which remain hostile to it will be deprived of investment and are placed at a disadvantage in inter-state competition, especially if they are coming late to the industrialization. They will tend to become poorer relative to their capitalist neighbors, leading to increasing internal dissatisfaction, fracturing of elites, and their likely overthrow by either internal or external foes.

The state is not, then, an eternal verity destined to contaminate all those who touch it but rather a site of struggle that reflects the balance of forces in wider society. It is a tool whose usefulness depends very much on who is wielding it and for what purpose. And like any technology, it has evolved in response to the external pressures applied to it so that in our era it both retains a similarity to its initial function (bash heads and extract the surplus) while accruing new functions and being significantly altered by these functions and the pressures which necessitated them.

Bourgeois Democracy

But even if the premise of the state as an intrinsically capitalist one does not hold up, there is the further issue of whether its form in the advanced capitalist countries is so antithetical to socialism that it is of little use in the project of socialist transformation. But what is this form? Leninist critics often describe it as 'bourgeois democracy' and therefore not a real form of democracy at all. If that view is correct, then the case for insurrection is more or less made, with only the tactical question of whether an insurrection can be carried off at a given juncture being at issue.

But is that view correct?

Socialism arose as a political doctrine in the 19th Century, a period in which there weren't any democracies by today's standards of universal suffrage and freedom to organize. Indeed the most advanced democratic country, the United States, was engaged in mopping up its anti-indigenous cleansing operations and still had slavery until the 1860s, followed by another century of legal discrimination. In Europe, the situation was different, but not much better. The Continent was dominated by monarchical governments and the major powers, Prussia, Austria, and Russia were governed by absolutist regimes that were removed from democratic influence. Even France, the centre of revolutionary hope for most of the this period, was governed by monarchical and imperial regimes for the bulk of the century. The other major power, England, while more liberal was not much more democratic. Apart from the obvious and still remembered exclusion of women, workers were denied participation in the political process in the 1830s and did not begin to make headway against this legal discrimination until 1867 and there were still restrictions against them as late as 1918.

Restrictions on Workers' Power

Under those conditions, the right of workers to organize themselves was highly circumscribed. In England, the Combination Acts legally restricted the ability to organize, although by the 1870s momentum was turning in the trade unions' favor. Not to be outdone, France under Louis Napoleon clamped down on worker organizations, enabling the anti-union philosophy of Proudhon to gain a foothold. The situation was naturally worse in less developed Germany, with the Social Democratic Party itself being banned by Bismarck in 1878 until his fall from power in the early 1890s while a thoroughly rigged electoral system persisted in Prussia right up until the revolution of 1918. The restrictions in Czarist Russia are widely known: suffice it to say that it was so antiquated and that freedom of organization was so restricted by its decaying feudal regime that even large sections of the bourgeoisie were revolutionary.

And these were just the overt, publicly declared discriminations against workers. There are many more instances of the state simply backing employers in labor disputes even to the extent of shooting at mass demonstrations. So, throughout the period in which modern socialism was emerging there were legal restrictions, even in otherwise fairly liberal countries, on the right of workers to organize and, consequently, their ability to win political power. Workers could hardly gain a majority in parliament when they were denied the vote.

The absence of democracy cannot be overcome by purely democratic means if only because of the absence of those means. The origins of modern socialism in an era of undemocratic states ensured that, just like many of the nationalist movements that arose at that time, they tended to be revolutionary. Given that there was no democratic way to bring the regimes to heel, some sort of revolution was going to be needed to overthrow them.

The disdain for 'bourgeois' democracy, although inherent in the original Anarchist position, became widespread amongst revolutionary socialists in the wake of the Lenin's break with the Marxist Centre through his gigantic gamble on the soviet horse and the resulting flood of Bolshevik polemics.

But the whole depiction of democracy as 'bourgeois' is entirely unhelpful, not to mention inaccurate. So-called bourgeois or formal democracy consists of universal suffrage, the rule of law, civic equality, the freedom to organize, elementary civil liberties and so forth. Essential as democracy is to socialism, it's not a purely socialist demand. Lots of other groups in society have an interest in the progressive democratization of society, including minority groups, females, and even the bourgeoisie and capitalists, whose freedom to accumulate is severely constrained if the state is strong enough to operate the law in an arbitrary fashion.

Democracy Is Required

For socialists, however, the importance of democracy goes further: apart from being intrinsically desirable in themselves, democratic freedoms are necessary if we are to organize large organizations at all because millions of people cannot unite as members of free institutions unless there is the ability to democratically set the fundamental policy (the constitution, the core program), elect, supervise and if necessary hold its leadership to account; if we cannot organize to propagate new ideas and fresh criticism and finally if there are legal restrictions on their right to do so in the first place. Democratic rights are a precondition – the light and air, as the orthodox Marxists put it – for a successful mass socialist movement to exist at all. Socialism is a project of collective emancipation and this requires the support and participation of those who are to be liberated.

The elementary rights of freedom of association, organization and so forth are therefore not bugs in the capitalist system but features of any socially advanced society, which includes but is not limited to countries in which the capitalist mode of production is dominant.

The argument that democracy is a rigged game because of the preponderance of wealth that the capitalist class can throw onto the scales is true but vacuous. That is a problem of capital ownership, not a problem of democracy. The cultural influence of capital doesn't just vanish if an electoral system based on representative democracy is replaced by some alternative form of democracy as is shown by both the strange street revolutions occurring in the Ukraine or the victory of the nationalist leadership of the SPD in the workers' councils elections in Germany in 1918.

If it is a problem of democracy, let us not shrink from the logical conclusion: since the vast majority of the population are workers, the very same distorting affect of wealth will intrude on the purity of the democratic process irrespective of the form used in that process, irrespective of whether we call it a state or a federation of workers councils or grassroots assemblies. A temporary dictatorship will be necessary to bridge the gap between the collapse of capitalist political power and the institution of a new mode of production, a gap that may well last some decades. Trotsky, at least in the early to mid 1920s, was honest enough to accept the logical endpoint of his insurrectionary strategy but modern insurrectionaries are not so forthright, no doubt because they believe that the process of revolution itself radicalizes the population to such a degree that the muck of capitalist propaganda is purged from their minds.

Rapture by Rupture

The problem is not with democracy, it's with the fact that we're not winning the battle of democracy. Since we are not legally prevented from winning, as the early socialists were, insurrection is a solution to the wrong problem. The real problems of the disparity of resources thrown into the cultural battle to gain majority support and the structural dependence of the state — and labor for that matter — on continuing capitalist investment, require quite a different solution.

Insurrectionary socialists place themselves in a bind: democracy is a fraud because of the unequal distribution of wealth in capitalist societies and the socialization of wealth is impossible because democracy is a fraud. Their solution is the catastrophic collapse of capitalism leading to the rapid destruction of the existing political system and the swift expropriation of private property. This is simply a modern, secular, version of the rapture in which the real problem of ownership of capital is solved by pushing it into an imaginary future in which the working class, deified as the risen Messiah, delivers salvation to humanity. Ironically, it was this very approach to which Marxism — aka scientific socialism — arose in opposition. After all, there were no shortage of socialist predecessors and competitors to Marxism, and many of them, such as syndicalism, had quite the following at one stage.

Subordination not Smashing is the Order of the Day

A further reason for not smashing the existing state is that we need it. The early 20th century state was already an old, complex bureaucratic entity, stretching back centuries and conquering it rather than destroying it was the aim of the European Socialist parties; indeed it was the divisive issue between them and the Anarchists. The modern state is needed for the simple reason that it performs socially necessary functions without which a technologically advanced, densely populated society would collapse. And compared to the pre WW I state, today's one runs vastly more essential services like healthcare, education, food and pharmaceutical safety regulation, environmental controls, provision of infrastructure, and a civil and criminal justice system.

If those functions go unfulfilled by a future socialist polity, the day-to-day experience of life for everyone will quickly degrade leading to an erosion of support for the socialist government (or polity). Court summonses for drink driving, to take just one example, will have to be issued under a socialist administration just as much as they would under a capitalist one. In theory, the state justice system can be replaced by popular tribunals but rules of procedure, expertise in summarizing and arguing the law, administrative clerks and the like cannot just be recreated at will. The legal norms are the product of a long, messy, and less than edifying social evolutionary process. Limited as they may be, they have the under-appreciated virtue of actually existing — not a trivial accomplishment. The difficulties which recently cropped up in English Trotskyism have given rise to much comment about the inadequacies of the left in dealing with sexual assault cases. But they also point to the sheer difficulty of developing a viable alternative to the state justice system. Popular tribunals must fulfill those legal functions better than the old legal system if the new system is to secure legitimacy. In practice, that is extremely hard to accomplish and it is worth asking, does each administrative function need to be recreated from scratch? The question becomes all the more urgent when asked in the midst of an intense confrontation with the ruling class.

A better approach is to think about how the existing systems can be improved, principally through the extension of democracy into the apparatus, e.g. by removing the veto power of the Supreme Court or making their terms of definite duration and subject to the democratic wishes as expressed by the various political parties. Rather than destroying a useful machine we want to subordinate it for our purposes.

A Protracted Task

Learning to guide a large bureaucracy into a democratic mode of operation is a herculean task and not one that can be learned on the fly over a few weeks or months of insurrection. It takes years if not decades. In times past, the trade unions were a vital source of practical knowledge in administration but these have significantly less reach than they used to. It's not a question of workers' capability but of organization, because it is only in certain forms of organization and under certain conditions that their capacity is actually realized.

A strategy of extending democracy under the auspices of the political party reduces the level of social reorganization that has to occur simultaneously if a confrontation with the capitalist class ever comes to a head. A large bureaucracy is a very complex machine and complex machines are far easier to break than to improve; the latter requires knowledge that tells us in advance that the change to be made is likely to increase the performance of the machine. Without such foreknowledge, any change is essentially random, and since there are vastly more ways for changes to degrade, if not wreck, the machine, changes which haven't been carefully thought through in advance can quickly lead to severe social crisis.

The State and Socialization

But extending democratization within the state is only part of the party's mission. It is of no use to have an unblemished tool which is admired but not used. As well as being the indispensable core of administering collective decision making, the state is a tool in the socialization process. The most vital change is the co-ordination of investment. With the division of labor becoming ever more international the need for ever more intricate co-ordination arises, and the more complex that co-ordination the less able institutional forms — let alone consciously anti-institutional forms— that emerge spontaneously in the revolutionary process will be capable of mastering it. The resulting break in the chain of production will see a severe decline in living standards and an immediate, perhaps irrevocable, plummeting of political support for seeing the transition out.

The precise form that socialization takes will vary according to circumstance, but in all cases the state, as both the overall sovereign authority and the vehicle for democratic participation must be at its centre. This does not necessarily entail an all pervasive level of control. For example, the state could mandate various banks to invest according to certain criteria which have won support through the majority socialist party.

It can also create, by using its legislative and judicial functions in a pro-labor way, a context which promotes workers' self-activity. The dead hand of state compulsion has been a longstanding worry amongst socialists and the economic stagnation of the USSR indicates it has a real basis in fact. How then can state involvement with socialization be coupled with self-activity? By tilting the playing field in favor of workers activity, e.g. by specifying a legal right to the products of their labor[3] or by permitting businesses to be transformed into co-operatives with public financing if a majority of workers vote for it, the state makes it in workers' own material interest to aggressively pursue socialization rather than stop at a welfare-state type solution.

In the first example above, workers would not be handed the products; the socialist militants would still have to persuade the workers in each enterprise to seek their legal right. Independent jury tribunals can decide in these and other cases between employers and worker. Assuming the juries are randomly selected, as they are now, then the working class will make up its majority, thereby facilitating pro-labor judgments. Of course, if the tribunals were to return consistently anti-labor decisions, we would have good evidence that support for socialization was waning and that a change in strategy is required. In any case, socialization is not being imposed from above against the wishes of the majority. Emanating from a democratically elected party and dependent on the daily support of workers to further the process, the development of a co-operative economy would rest on a very solid foundation of mass support. It can assume the burden of providing collective goods so that workers co-ops can operate at much lower cost level and therefore compete with capitalist companies.

Capitalist Reaction and The Security State

The public sector is not populated by ogres, who become instruments of capital simply because of their role in the bureaucracy or due to some as yet unknown consequences of its particular form. Their specific role depends on a host of factors, not least the requirements of its own reproduction. To the extent that the apparatus depends on continued investment by capitalists in the economy, it has no choice but to align its interests with that of the capitalist class. But should another mode of production — producer co-operatives — begin to appear as a threatening cloud on the horizon, the apparatus has no intrinsic loyalty to capitalism for it is not itself a capitalist entity. To be sure, there will be personal loyalties, especially at the higher echelons who, having gone to the same posh schools, will be horrified at the thought of the plebs taking over.

Should they begin to disrupt the socialization policy of democratically chosen socialist party they will have to be neutralized and replaced by more well disposed individuals. What is of more importance is that the vast bulk of public sector workers, including the administrative workers in the Civil Service, are onside with a policy of socialization. Only a mass party with roots throughout the community, with an organizational reach comparable to the Catholic Church of old, can hope to win the active and passive support from the bureaucracy which is necessary to carry through socialization measures.

Nevertheless, it would hardly be surprising if elements within the apparatus attempt to disrupt the necessary structural reforms, e.g. taking control of credit, altering labor legislation in favor of trade unions and co-operatives etc. As it is, the bureaucracy stymies existing pro-capitalist governments all the time. We can expect degrees of co-operation within the state apparatus which itself will not be unaffected by the balance of forces in society generally. A rise in support for the socialist party and the increasing competitiveness of worker co-ops will enable sympathetic tendencies within the apparatus to be more vocal and to push those sitting on the fence to co-operate while resisting the disruptive efforts of the recalcitrants. But the sympathetic tendency requires direction from a legitimate government sanctioned by a democracy.

By winning the battle for democracy, we make it harder for the holdouts in the state to organize resistance. Reactionary pro-capitalist elements that attempt to disrupt socialization will find their options have narrowed considerably once they find they have lost the co-operation of great swathes of the administrative apparatus itself while legitimacy and sheer numbers enhances the position of our allies, making it easier for them to argue for co-operation with the socialization project. We must make it easy for them to comply with socialization and make it costly for them to block it.

At some point the reactionaries will try to move onto more aggressive measures, including investment strikes and ultimately a coup d'état. We won't deal with the inevitable investment pressure that will be brought to bear other than to say if the socialist movement hasn't prepared the ground well in advance by having sufficient weight in the productive sector that it can see out such a strike, then it can simply forget about instigating any structural reforms that take us in a socialist direction.

Should the socialist-labor movement prove too resilient to fold before the disruption aimed at fostering economic breakdown, the doomsday weapon of violent reaction, whether through the mobilization of a mass fascist movement or via a straight-forward coup d'état always looms over its head, ready to detonate. This sober fact is one of the common reasons cited by insurrectionaries when arguing for the need to smash the state itself. Unfortunately, however, while destruction may solve the problem of the military reserve option for the ruling class, it doesn't, as we argued above, solve the problem of being able to transition to a socialist mode of production.

And nor is it the best to counter the possibility of violent reaction. Just as democratic legitimacy is a counter to the recalcitrant bureaucracy within the civil service, it is also a weapon against those sections of the state, i.e. the security state (the political police, the intelligence agencies, the officer corps). Again, it enhances the possibility of a split within the ranks of larger security agencies, i.e. those with lots of members with ordinary functions. Many of the great revolutionary events in history, including decisive movements in the French and Russian Revolutions, were settled by the refusal of the rank and file soldiers to fire on protestors. The more we have legitimacy the easier we make it for them to disobey their reactionary officers, especially as there will likely splits within the security state, with some of their leaders having internalized the values of liberal democracy, will maintain their loyalty to the legitimate line of authority.

Put the Burden on the Ruling Class

Of course, should the democratic process itself come under attack, either through a frontal coup d'état or through a prolonged form of technocratic government installed by the IMF or the ECB, then an old-fashioned street revolution becomes not only desirable but inevitable. Until that scenario occurs, however, we need to approach the question of revolution from a defensive standpoint. As Engels put it, it's tactically in our interests to put the ruling class in the position of having to shoot first as they would have to bear the burden of responsibility for being anti-democratic, while socialists get to be defenders of not only egalitarianism but of democracy too, thereby making it easier to split potential allies, such as small businesses, off from the right-wing. As the experience of the last century has shown the far left, it is not so easy to organize insurrection against a democratically elected government, especially in the advanced capitalist countries.

Nor is revolution itself an inherently positive development. A fair proportion of history's revolutions have had little progressive content, e.g. the anti-French revolt of the Spanish in the revolutionary era, while more modern mass protests regularly veer close to being essentially the useful idiots of the American foreign policy establishment – the anti-Chavez protests of 2002 being the clearest example. In Ireland, the grassroots Ulster Workers' Councils of the mid-1970s, which led to the shutdown of the province, was entirely reactionary in nature.

A good example of the limited value of street insurrections as a gauge of progressive content is the enthusiasm which led the (Cliffite) SWP to both endorse the Muslim Brotherhood when it was benefitting from the overthrow of Mubarak and to oppose it when its democratically elected government was the subject of a military led street revolution. Rather than promote a long-term strategy of building organizations capable of outcompeting both the Muslim Brotherhood and the military they preferred to take the shortcut of insurrection. In the end, however, the shortcuts lead nowhere, since there is no shortcut to building up mass, popular organizations, the measure of which is victory in democratic elections. Neither the secular-liberals nor the socialists, both of whom lack institutions on the scale of the Muslim Brotherhood, are capable of mounting a challenge to win popular support on the scale of the Islamists and so street revolutions end up in the entirely reactionary laps of the military establishment.

Conclusion of Part One

Just as with a strategy of insurrection, there are political implications to attempting to conquer political power and subordinate the state to the process of socialization. We can summarize those implications thus:

1. Subordination requires support both active and passive support within the apparatus.

2. Democratic legitimacy is essential to securing that support.

3. Democratic legitimacy means winning power democratically and putting that legitimacy to the test repeatedly.

4. Winning elections requires a mass party.

So arising from our position on the state, a quite different conception of political strategy follows. On the one hand, insurrection with a revolutionary vanguard party and mass assemblies, on the other, mass socialist parties winning power via the existing democratic system. Or, to put the argument another way, if we don't need an insurrection and if we don't need an entirely new system of workers councils, we don't require parties whose fundamental task is to promote that strategy. Because we are making socialism and not insurrection the central strategic goal, we have no need to maintain an organizationally distinct revolutionary party.

Quite the opposite. We want to merge the socialists into mass organizations so that ideologically socialist parties exist on a truly large basis over a prolonged period of time, for decades at least, for centuries if necessary.

Notes to Part One

1. The idea is most clearly and poetically expressed by Trotsky: "the history of a revolution is for us first of all the forcible entrance of the masses into the realm of their own destiny".

2. We elaborate on this interpretation of capitalist domination in *Science and Socialism*.

3. These examples follow the lines of thought of Cockshott, Cottrell, & Dieterich in their *Transition to 21st Century Socialism in the European Union*.

Part II: Extra Ecclesiam nulla salus (Outside of the Church there is no Salvation)

Emancipation through Organization

In order for strategies to become more permanently established they need to be theorized. Just as the Leninists, from 1919 on, theorized the de facto dictatorship of the Bolshevik party into the theological knots of vanguardism and the Anarchists theorized the workers councils as the vehicle of liberation, Kautsky and the Marxist Center theorized the mass socialist-labor organizations as the agents of socialist transformation. The view was brought out in the debates between Otto Bauer and Kautsky over the USSR in the 1920s and 1930s. Bauer argued that there could be a Russian road to socialism; that the backward conditions found there facilitated the crash-course of industrialization which would pave the way for socialism in the future.

For Kautsky this was illusion. Socialism does not arise from industrialization per se. It comes from the action of the working class, action which can only occur via their own free, independent organizations. And it was precisely these which were absent in the USSR, with only one legal political party, trade unions which were under its tutelage, and a pervasive political police.

For sure, a technically advanced country was the precondition for the very possibility of an urban working class, never mind a working class organized into its own institutions. Before capitalism the masses existed in a permanent state of subordination broken only by sporadic and doomed uprisings, inherently incapable of instituting a socialist mode of production.

Class struggle of a Different Kind

The creation, through the expansion of capitalist production, of the urban working class provoked a new and qualitatively different round of the class struggle: not, this time, between the bourgeoisie and the aristocracy, but between capitalism's creation, the modern proletariat, and the capitalist class itself. And it was the class struggle that arose from capitalist industrialization that forced the working class to organize its own trade unions, its own co-operatives, and, eventually, its own political party. It was to be through these institutions — so went the narrative of Second International Marxism — that the working class would build such hegemonic influence that it could win state power and transform society by transforming the mode of production.

If a large political party is a prerequisite for gaining control of the state, large worker organizations are also a precondition of socialism. Without organization, the working class is just an amorphous mass of individuals, at the mercy of capitalist command of resources and its torrents of propaganda. It is only through organization that it becomes an active player. And without organizations we cannot organize labor on a mass basis. If the First International's famous slogan proclaimed that the emancipation of the workers would the be the task of the workers themselves, the Second International's variation amounted to "the emancipation of the workers is the task of the workers' organizations". Not as pithy, but more specific.

In the absence of mass socialist-labor institutions workers' capacity for action is restricted to protest and destruction. Kautsky, in the debates with Luxemburg, was explicit about the limitations of unorganized mass actions, i.e. spontaneous actions that were not coordinated by specific institutions. These type of action are restricted, they're only defensive or destructive political actions, i.e. they could bring down a regime (as they did in February 1917) but they could not in themselves construct an alternative to the existing order except through the workers' own political party and, critically for the project of raising a socialist mode of production to dominance, via co-ops and labor unions. Spontaneous action was by no means rendered redundant by the rise of the labor organizations; under certain conditions, essentially extremely repressive conditions such as existed in Tsarist Russia, or indeed in the final toppling of the Kaiser, it played an indispensable role. It also served to act as a reserve weapon against the capitalist class should it force the labor movement into a smaller and smaller space of legal existence.

But to go beyond the mere destruction of a conservative force, the organizations needed to exist and to exist on a mass scale while being imbued with a socialist, and preferably Marxist, ideology. To be sure, socialists could not bring about the revolution at will. There were much larger social forces at play: the erosion by industrialization of the feudal remnants; geo-political maneuvering; the pace of technological developments, etc. But socialists could control what they did with their own organizations. They could choose to pursue a purist revolutionary line and dispense with the mass worker organizations or they could choose to focus on direct economic action, as advocated by the syndicalists. In Kautsky's view, they needed to prioritize the building of their own organizations and wait for the dynamics of capitalist development to deliver opportunities for winning power, an approach he called "the strategy of attrition".

Contra Pannekoek, who viewed the strategy of attrition as in effect a form of "actionless waiting", it was not going to be a passive affair. It involved a continuous strengthening of the movement institutions: more recruitment into the labor unions and strengthening their capacity for struggle; more and larger co-ops; increasing the membership and popularity of the party and its related cultural clubs; deepening the socialist intellectuals' understanding of economics, the materialist conception of history, and expanding the reach of the socialist publications, etc. In sum, it involved the construction and continual expansion of a socialist ecosystem of organizations which could withstand the considerable pressure brought to bear by their capitalist and aristocratic opponents. Hence the title, the strategy of attrition.

Having outlined, nay bludgeoned, the importance of socialist organizations we are in a position to identify the role of electoralism. On their own, elections don't put us on the road to socialism; they just do what the Trotskyists always accuse the Marxist minimum program of doing: of making capitalism more tolerable — an under-appreciated virtue to be sure, but in any case a different one to what we are trying to achieve. It is only as a component part of the strategy of attrition that electoralism plays a critical part in moving beyond capitalism. Winning power is therefore not the only goal of electoralism; every bit as important is the role it plays in building a mass socialist party capable of winning it and of controlling the apparatus when it gets there.

Mass Organizations as a Fetter?

For the supporters of council (soviet) democracy and the vanguard insurrectionary party, this is an entirely redundant approach. If anything the creation of permanent mass institutions becomes a fetter which prevents a revolutionary overthrow of capitalism by the treacherous actions of its bureaucratized leadership when the hour strikes. But for the Marxist Centre, as the proponents of the attrition strategy were known, the task of building up the organizations is the heart of all socialist activity. Not only should elections be seen in this light, but so too should demonstrations, leaflets, pickets, participating in single-issue campaigns and basically everything else we do.

Pannekoek and Luxemburg misjudged two factors. They overestimated the ease with which radical or direct action could escalate into revolution and they underestimated the importance of building the mass socialist-labor organizations. In a way this was understandable. Very significant gains, especially in the extension of suffrage, were being made in the aftermath of the Russian Revolution and, secondly, they had come to political maturity in an environment in which mass socialist organizations were a feature of social life. They were taken for granted. The issue, from their perspective, was to set these organizations in motion. But from our perspective, a century later, and having witnessed the eclipse of all varieties of socialist parties in the advanced capitalist states, it is the absence or severe weakness of mass organizations that is the problem, not that they are too conservative. Recreating them is not a trivial problem. There are no shortage of Luxemburgist alternatives, i.e. radical attempts at street demonstrations, from the anti-WTO protests of Seattle to the Occupy movement of 2011. But they have proved to be no panacea and when capitalism tottered in September 2008 there wasn't the slightest question that there was an alternative economic system that could step in and immediately take over. The strategy of attrition, of building up the mass socialist-labor institutions, is designed to solve that problem.

Eco-system Resilience and Virtuous Cycles - Cumulative Growth

The emphasis on the long-term building of mass organizations carries with it a number of key benefits. Take media, which are indispensable if we are to compete with capitalism for ideological dominance since that is how public communication to vast numbers of people occurs. We need funds to organize media, not just newspapers but television stations, websites, iPhone apps and the like. It costs money to pay journalists, sub-editors, programrs, and designers. We lack the capital but we have the numbers, an advantage that is only realized when we are organized. The potential volume of small contributions is immense and while it may not match what is available to the capitalists, it would certainly enable us to promote a socialist worldview at a mass level and enter in serious competition with the ruling class.

The German Social Democratic party had a myriad of social clubs: it had its own media apparatus, selling a million copies a week and with many more readers. It had theoretical journals, but it also had summer camps, athletic clubs, cycling clubs, even smoking clubs. The Italian Communists existed at a similar level. What they had in effect was an entire eco-system of organizations.

These don't necessarily lead to radicalism, but they do lead to the organizations planting deep, deep roots in society. In many ways, they created something that is closer to a secular church than to a mere political party, and they reaped the benefit of the emotional attachment that their members had for the movement so that even a prolonged period of fascist reaction could not uproot them from society.

Once socialist institutions reach a critical mass a positive feedback loop kicks in. Our media normalizes the idea of a co-operative economy, which leads to passive support, more donations, more votes, and more activists which leads to an increase in services: new worker co-ops, mutual aid funds, social clubs, choirs and so on. These further project the viability of socialism as a movement and an ideology which leads to further support, more donations, the surplus from the co-ops going to fund the party, which promotes the general idea of socialism through its increasing resources and so on in a positive feedback loop. A process of ratcheting up is underway, leading to a virtuous cycle in which cumulative gains are now possible.

Insurrection and the Single Issue Campaign

In contrast, insurrectionary political parties are not at all oriented to working that way. Their primary strategic approach is to engage in federalist political coalitions (sometimes over-theorized as a united front) or, more commonly, single-issue campaigns in loose alliances with other far left groups and assorted independents. Whatever the obligation to engage in single-issues campaigns — and they are just a fact of political life — these campaigns rarely get beyond that particular issue itself. So, when that campaign is over, irrespective of whether it has ended in victory or defeat, the next campaign must start from the same low basis, lacking internal infrastructure and the political equivalent of brand awareness. The coordinating mechanisms must be constructed from scratch. As a single-issue campaign, it must stick fairly closely to the issue at hand or risk alienating the non-political people who are just concerned about it and not the wider political situation.

But there is no cumulative benefit because the organizations are different. The supporters who engage with the issue of unfair tax might have very little interest in an oil pipeline in Alaska. In order to benefit from the cumulative process of individual campaigns, there needs to be continuity of organization so that when the next issue comes up, we are starting from a more advanced point.

The insurrectionary strategy fails badly at this and in fact revolutionary parties are not set up to take advantage of the often Trojan work they do behind the scenes in these campaigns because they don't want to build mass non-revolutionary parties. So, for them, it's not even a major problem as their strategy relies on an outbreak of revolutionary upheaval rather than incremental growth of organizations as the vehicle of social transformation.

Unfortunately, it's simply not possible to get big and capable institutions in one go. Even in highly favorable circumstances, there has to be a pre-existing institution that is set up to take advantage of it, which takes time to get its internal organizational structure and external strategy into presentable shape. It is necessary, therefore, to adopt a strategy that enables cumulative growth and that entails, by definition, having institutions which persist through time. But in the vanguard model the most long-lasting organization is the revolutionary party which is precisely the one that is least able to grow to a considerable size. It is only the ephemeral single-issue campaigns and ideologically fluffy alliances which are able to achieve major proportions and they, because of what they are, are structurally incapable of persisting through time, thereby preventing any possibility of cumulative growth. As long, therefore, as the radical left maintains its current division between revolutionary and mass organizations it will be incapable of ever attaining the strength to implement its program of socialization.

In contrast, the classical Marxist approach of merging the socialist intelligentsia with the mass labor movement to form a socialist-labor movement provides a way out of the inability to either never grow large enough or for the mass organizations to be bereft of a socialist ideology. This "merger formula" is the conception that undergirds the strategy of attrition just as theory of the vanguard party fits snugly into a strategy of insurrection.

Political Consequences

Electoralism is the most important political activity in the European and North American societies and in practice it forms the centerpiece of activity for the remaining mass socialist-labor parties, such as Syriza in Greece, the French Communists and so on. Although putting the party and its program to the test in elections is the priority it doesn't preclude a host of other activities, including involvement in single-issue campaigns. In practice these will take up a lot of time just as they do now for the radical left. But in order to benefit from electoral work there has to be an institutionalization of the gains, whether through increased participation in the party or union, more subscriptions to sympathetic left-wing media, joining a co-op or simply voting for the party come election time. These and other possible methods of harvesting the labor expended in the springtime of campaigning all depend on having institutions capable of soaking up the goodwill.

Organization enables a sort of alchemy; the transmutation of goodwill into support and practical activity over the long term. Mass parties (and associated organs, co-ops, etc.) are not just admirably suited to achieving this, they are absolutely necessary. For every cadre member who

joins a revolutionary party, there will be thousands more who are sympathetic to the basic goals of socialism. An emphasis on the destructive
side of socialism, i.e. one which focuses on the necessity to smash the
state, makes it harder for these potential sympathizers to participate
in the movement in a sustained, long-term way, if only because of its
intrinsic lack of plausibility. And even where single-issue campaigns are
necessary, which seems likely to be the case for a long time to come,
a socialist electoral party has no need to hide its politics in the initial
period and then rush to spray them all over the campaign when it looks
like it's coming to an end.

Politics of the Strategy of Attrition

The strategy of attrition is, therefore, compatible with a type of politics
that is close to where many people already are. Its radicalism lies in its
goals, not in its practice and this makes it easier to interact with non-
socialists on an open basis. There is no need to hide its insurrectionary
orientation because it doesn't have one. As long as the party has a pro-
grammatic commitment to a co-operative mode of production and uses
other avenues, e.g. its media or its public representatives, to articulate
that, its mere presence as an ally of campaigns is enough to raise awareness of its goals.

In political terms, it requires genuinely engaging in electoral politics with
the aim of winning since that is both the route to democratically gaining
power and the best way of achieving large size in the political realm. It's
often argued that engagement with electoralism detracts from the core
message of promoting socialism, as more immediate concerns, including the need to get re-elected, crowd out the longer term vision. This
is a valid insight, but the assumption that ignoring the immediate ways
people interact with politics doesn't solve it. It just results in even less
opportunity to engage with folks about any sort of politics at all.

For sure, at the micro level, the focus on the day-to-day is inevitable.
It is, however worth taking a broad and long, i.e. decades long, view
of its function. People aren't going to be won over to socialism from
a few chats at a door or a round of public talks. Shifting people's values, consciousness, and tribal loyalties is a complex process. But each
interaction can be a contribution to a movement gaining credibility. Every iteration of positive, even neutral contact between socialists and Joe
Public chips away at the negative assumptions inculcated by the wider
culture. But, more than that, electoral participation and victory conveys
the impression of a competent organization and as low-level messages
for socialism seep through, the idea becomes normalized. Electoral vali-
dation helps create a culture where socialism can be discussed.

Now, for micro-interactions to be a contribution, they have to be a contribution to something. And something with an ability to scale. Promulgating revolutionary insurrection, smashing the state, etc., does not at all mix with chatting to Mary about the cut to child benefit. On the other hand, where there is a pre-existing movement that projects a grander vision, then each iteration of micro-contact about non-revolutionary issues serves to normalize that movement and therefore its vision. Clearly there is a danger that the day-to-day concerns force the grand vision into the background. Such is the risk of engaging with reality. But without being able to relate the day-to-day with the long-term project, the proponents of socialism will remain very isolated intellectuals.

The more that our activists can make the connection between the two the better, but as anyone who has had experience knows, it's damn hard to get up in a workplace staff meeting about overcrowding in the canteen and make the connection with global capitalism. The same applies for potholes on country roads or traffic calming measures in the city centre. Occasionally a gap will open and the activist can make a punt about generalizing the inadequacies to the economic system itself, but usually it will make you look a bit strange, especially if that opening is forced, in which case it can actually be counter-productive (which is one reason why those American Spartacists come across as really bizarre in many of their public interventions).

Promoting Socialism

The task of promoting socialism — the collectivization of the economy, co-operatives, etc. — will be made much easier for the grassroots activists the more that our intellectuals and prominent party members (MPs, etc.) can articulate it in a defensible manner. The starting point for this cannot be the mass media, which confines you to soundbites or at most a critique bereft of the opportunity of addressing structural issues, such as the ownership of the means of production. To even utter the phrase "the means of production" would probably take up half your response time on pretty much all mainstream current affairs programs.

That battle takes place at a different level and the MPs get a simplified message, e.g. democratic control of investment, promotion of co-ops. Even then, most of their opportunities for interaction with the public will be on non-socialist issues, corruption, waste, war, civil rights (including gender equality, solidarity with immigrants, etc.). Every time they do well on these issues they increase the probability that the economic message is taken seriously. The more that happens, the easier it is for the grassroots activists to do the leg-work because the socialist vision is animating the movement as a whole. Thus, whatever strengthens the party / movement strengthens socialism, providing of course, the party continues to place socialization at the heart of the project.

The Costs of the Strategy of Attrition

But if the merger formula is vastly more likely to lead to success, it far from guarantees it. Although it solves the problem of never being able to get on a track of cumulative growth it does run into the very heavy problem of integration into the existing political-economic system. The fate of the German SPD and the Italian Communists is ample evidence of the seriousness of the problem. All actions have costs and the cost of a mass organization is a bureaucracy without which it cannot be maintained for more than a few months — not long enough to get the cumulative growth we need. When radical left groups are small they can persuade themselves that a distinct apparatus is unnecessary because for them it more or less is unnecessary. But that doesn't apply to groups with millions of members, which is the scale we need to be aiming for.

Bureaucracies may be necessary, but they are also dangerous as they have a tendency to escape the control of the membership. Their first duty is to preserve the organization itself and this leads to a conservative mentality. Again, this is unavoidable if the organization is to exist. A trade union which hurled its members onto the barricades at every opportunity would soon see itself reduced to a fringe group.

In addition to the natural tendency towards conservatism, mass organizations of socialist opposition will come under immense cultural pressure. Its members will be subject to pro-capitalist propaganda and won't be immune to the effects of the wider culture, which is massively suffused with capitalist values. Indeed, if socialists provided no other service than creating media capable of competing with the propaganda machines of the right, they would render an immense service to humanity.

The pressure of the wider pro-capitalist culture combined with the tendency towards increasing conservative apparatus makes the strategy of attrition a risky one. There is a race on between the socialist organizations aiming to transform capitalist society before capitalist society transforms them. The calculation is that the socialist-labor institutions can last long enough and make socialism an attractive enough ideology so that when the cracks appear in the capitalist edifice, they will be able to sweep in and begin restructuring the economy. But there is no question that the strategy of attrition courts integration if those cracks are patched up quickly enough. If the capitalist mode of production proves to be healthy over the long-term then it is likely these organizations will suffer the fate of the SPD or the PCI. But it puts us in the game; a game we might lose, but also one that we might win. Without the mass organizations the insurrectionary groups aren't even in the competition and so while they can't ever lose, they can't ever win either.

Socialists have an important role in the struggle against the domination of the apparatus of the movement itself. The battle for socialism must be won not only in wider society, but within the socialist party and within the co-operatives and trade unions, not just once, but year after year until socialism is the dominant mode of production. Encouraging the participation of the grassroots in the life of the party is also an essential feature in keeping the bureaucracy in its box. In recent years, a lot of thought has gone into new forms of democracy, e.g. liquid democracy, sociocracy, sortition, etc. While these are worth experimenting with, the chief weapons remain freedom to organize and the freedom to articulate criticism and dissent. Compared to them, the precise procedures that are used fade into second place. This freedom requires a party tolerant of diverse views and one that facilitates their expression through its own institutions, e.g. magazines, summer schools and the like. Provided the dissenters do not have an agenda of splitting the mass party, the dissent is likely to strengthen rather than weaken it.

Further, the existence of a wider eco-system of organizations promotes alternative material interests to that of the status quo. A leadership whose resources depend on funding from a vibrant co-operative or union movement will be constrained from throwing their lot in with capital.

Forms of Democracy

As this piece is centered on immediate strategy, it has focused on the two main choices: a vanguard party or a mass party. But as we saw, there is a second part to the insurrectionary equation and that is the mass assemblies, which are usually held up as a superior form of democracy to the 'bourgeois' form of the parliamentary systems.

There are many varieties of both systems, but the main differentiating feature lies in the conception of the role of the party as a mediating force or promoting the direct participation in the decision making process. That is, in current democratic systems, we vote for representatives who pass laws according to the strength of the party to which they belong. The criticism leveled at this type of system is that the representatives escape the control of the electors. The alternative is based on some form of assembly democracy in which the masses can participate directly. These federate and elect delegates to coordinating assemblies and if they cover a large enough territory these secondary councils do the same again, thereby forming a nested pyramid structure, all supported by the base assemblies. There are lots of problems with such a complicated system as is evidenced by the rarity in which they have been capable of supporting mass institutions, let alone being the basis of any state. Even at their height in the Russian Revolution, the assemblies (or soviets) only managed to exert significant social power for about 12 to 15 months.

As is often the case, the cure of assemblies is worse than the disease of partyism. Whereas partyism accepts that differences of opinion are based on real material interests, the assembly form, especially when it uses a form of consensus decision making, assumes the fundamental identity of interest amongst all the participants. The hostility to parties makes sense for proponents of the council form if differences of opinion are based on ignorance or bad faith. And that assumption is warranted in certain conditions: in sects such as the Quakers in which the membership do have, more or less, the same worldview and the same belief in the power of supernatural inspiration it is quite workable.

In politics, however, life is more complicated. Getting past capitalism is an incredibly difficult problem to which there are often no obvious solutions. At the outbreak of mass protest or revolution this is not a problem since the issue presents itself to the opposition in a simple way, e.g. "down with the regime", "against the 1%", "they all must go" (Argentina 2001). Sooner or later, however, it becomes necessary to move beyond a simple formulation of the problem and to advance structural solutions. This is hard for a number reasons, not least the number of variables that have to be taken into consideration. Because of that it becomes difficult to predict the consequences of any given policy.

Climate as a Case in Point

For instance, given the looming problem of climate change, should we develop an energy infrastructure based around nuclear power instead of wind and solar power? Nuclear could solve the energy problem once and for all, but it could also lead to a loss of social cohesion if it is unpopular due to safety concerns. Wind and Solar might not be able to solve the looming climate change problem given the relatively paltry power generation capabilities they have, but perhaps if they were made the keystone of our climate strategy, investment would flow to research and development which would lead to them catching up with nuclear. Society has only a limited capacity to invest in energy infrastructure so it has to make a choice between them. Even experts do not have a consensus around it for the simple reason it's a tricky problem.

It is hard to predict the consequences of any given policy but the difficulty escalates exponentially when we attempt to understand the the consequences of the consequences. It's not that nobody is thinking about it, it's just that the only problems we can solve are the ones presented to us by the environment and since we have yet to trigger the process by implementing the first tier of solutions we have yet to be confronted by the altered environmental conditions to which they give rise, thereby making it hard to assess what issues will give rise to the new set of problems. Consciousness and science help for sure, but they do not remove this issue of 'future blindness'.

This problem is a fundamental one and has nothing to do with direct democracy or capitalism or even human nature.

And the energy problem is a fairly simple one to solve compared to the figuring out the likely issues arising out of socializing the means of production, taking control of investment and progressively reducing co-ordination of production via the market. Inevitably there will be different views on these issues in a way that there simply isn't regarding incontrovertible facts (the earth revolves on its axis; the Irish are drunken peasants).

We can only rely on the collective will of society as expressed, after prolonged discussion, by the majority. Irrespective of the procedural form of democracy we choose, people will come together to form coalitions around the major issues of the day as they are too important to not try and win a majority for one's own position. These coalitions will coalesce as people of similar values and intellectual orientation will find it easier to compromise with each other and form a stable alliance. This will give that group an advantage in its struggle with other coalitions as they will be better able to mobilize more support more often to back up its position. If the other coalitions are to stand a chance of having their views listened to, they will have to similarly form a stable enough formation that can garner a competitive level of support. In other words there will be a selective pressure for unity and the ability to be permanently aligned. And with the inevitable emergence of such tendencies we are right back at, in effect, a party system.

The absence of a systemic tolerance and utilization of tendencies (or factions or parties) does not result there being no distinct factions at all. This is impossible since they reflect real differences in society. It just means that the dominant faction is the only one that is organized as such and this gives them a permanent advantage in the competition with other tendencies. If socialists refuse to organize its own organizations in a way that can outcompete the pro-capitalist parties, they will simply be swept away no matter how directly democratic the procedures are.

The assumption of underlying consensus is not just a mistake of the modern day radicals, inspired by Occupy or the 1960s New Left. Lenin, in The State and Revolution, consistently treats the working class, indeed the revolutionary population in general, as being of a unified mind. There is zero indication that he expects there to be a continual democratic struggle between tendencies for supremacy. One of the rare mentions of such a possibility is his offer prior to the October Revolution to be a sort of loyal opposition to the SRs and Mensheviks if the latter would take power via the soviets. But after that there is vanishingly little. The assumption that the councils would be of one mind and that that mind had vested the revolution to the Bolshevik Party led to, at first, intolerance of opposition — even socialist opposition — but eventually to outright repression of every organizational manifestation of opposition to the Bolshevik government.

But being of one mind is vastly unlikely when we are confronted with important issues and afflicted by future blindness. What if one tendency wants to pay compensation to the capitalists and another wants to expropriate them outright? Either the minorities can be expelled as occurred in the French and Russian Revolutions or the various tendencies can coalesce into parties, which strive to attain a majority.

If the expulsion route is followed, a major civil war is inevitable, not just between the right and the left, but within the left. The experiences of the Russian and Spanish Revolution indicate that this is a real possibility and progress to socialism will be delayed for a long time to come. Political differences are best fought out politically, in the open, and via democracy.

Elections Are Required

If there is to be democracy there will have to be periodic election to the assemblies. Those of a similar worldview will create organizations and strive to win a majority within the councils, which is what happened in Russia and everywhere else the council form broke out. If political parties are allowed, then we are essentially in the same position that we are now, albeit with a much more decentralized system, which if anything is vastly inferior for advancing towards a collectively run economy. And it is hardly worth the effort to stage an insurrection so that we can have elections to representative bodies which are dominated by political parties, when that is pretty much what we have already.[1]

Worse, the promotion of the council system goes hand-in-hand with a profoundly anti-political mindset that we see in the downplaying of the role of political parties. We see this in things like the Irish Occupy stuff of a couple years back where they'd object to political party banners on their demonstrations or asking members of political parties to participate in a personal capacity only. Again, Lenin, in his weird moment of anarchism when writing State and Revolution, captures that mentality:

the soviets are conceptualized as organs in which the decisions that workers have to make are administrative ones; they is no hint that there will be political decisions to be made. And with no politics, there is no need for multiple political parties.

In fact, from our point of view, we want politics to be conducted along party lines because we want there to be an openly socialist party with the aim of a co-operative mode of production. We want people to choose socialism and to know that they are choosing socialism, which is only possible if there are other parties espousing a different goal or even just a different route. We don't want them to fall into radicalism through engagement with street demonstrations that have snowballed into insurrection because they'll fall out of that radicalism just as quickly. Rather, an explicit choice to vote for and/or to become an active participant in the socialist movement is a much better indication of support for the socialization project.

Mass participation is, of course, a vital feature of any real democratic system, let alone a socialist one. But mass participation is best facilitated through organizations rather than in assemblies, especially assemblies with vague criteria for participating. The type of direct participation envisaged by the skeptics of parties and other mass organizations results in only the thinnest involvement in important decisions. The more people, the less that any one person's input matters. In order to have substantial influence we have to organize in smaller sub-groups which leverage their collective labor. In addition, in order for the division of labor between these sub-groups to not be wasted there needs to be co-ordination between them and sovereign authority (both for society at large, but also for a particular organization) that can make decisions when conflicts arise. Since it is important to keep the sovereign authority on a democratic leash, internal democracy — the freedom to organize articulate criticism, change policy, replace leaders, etc. — is required. This applies to the shibboleth of the radical socialism, the recall of delegates. As we are not proposing an assembly system, we don't wish the entirety of electorate to be able to exert a right of recall. Rather, control of the delegate should occur via the party: it should have the right of recall and if voters wish to exert that level of control, which would of course be welcome, they should join a party of a similar ideological disposition and be active within that.

There is nothing mystical about party forms of organization which necessarily prevents the exercise of mass control over its representatives and leaderships. It mainly requires participation and the ability to dissent and there is no reason that mass organizations should be inferior to nebulous forms likes base assemblies in either of those. And the greater the degree of participation by the membership the more dependent the representatives will be on them, thus making it easier to exert control over them.

Not only is a mass party and the existing democratic system a superior strategy for dealing with the issue of the state, it also a more sustainable one democratically speaking because it is capable of lasting much longer than the initial period of revolutionary enthusiasm. The obverse of the mass participation of 1917 is the mass apathy of the 1920s, which led Trotsky to justify the dictatorship of the party.

We argued above that there is good reason to be cautious about changing extremely complex entities like a state bureaucracy. Nevertheless, it is worth considering improvements and the socialist organizations can be experimental grounds for figuring out what new procedural forms can actually function in mass institutions. So, something like sortition could be utilized for an internal party parliament which exercises oversight on the leadership between conferences.

Despite the shortcomings of parliamentary democracy, it remains the best gauge of public support for a political tendency. A socialist society depends on the support of the majority of the people, and that support needs to be publicly recognizable, i.e. it supporters and opponents alike agree that a socialist government has a mandate to implement its program. The widespread acceptance of democracy as an organizing principle gives socialism the chance of becoming the dominant political force in a country and of validating its actions in the transition. In fact, if the electoral system didn't exist, it would be necessary to invent it.

The Coming Upheaval and Copernican Socialism

One of the elegant features of orthodox Marxism was its insight that the dynamic of capitalist expansion would lead to its eventual downfall. Capitalism, however, is still in expansionary mode, eating up the rural reserve of labor in Asia, pursuing the commodification of public services in Europe, and advancing technological development across the world. As long as it remains this dynamic it is going to be hard to surpass in productivity, especially given the level of co-operative production we are starting from. But if it is still expanding, it is also running into difficulties, as the problems in finding profitable investment opportunities over the last five years attests.

As capitalism develops and the means of production rise to ever more advanced levels, it must also progress the automatization of the labor process, thereby squeezing the working class of its income and capitalist firms of their customers. Combined with the imminent ending of the rural reserve of labor and the increasing problems that workers, especially highly qualified ones, will have in finding opportunities for social advancement within the existing system, we can expect more and more working people to develop ideas of radical opposition.

Add in the pressure of climate change, increasing geo-political rivalry, and the severe rises in inequality it is conceivable that instability on a scale not seen since the early 20th century could return. At the very least, with transition to an information economy, there will be opportunities for socialist production to demonstrate its superiority which is a precondition to winning mass support for socialism itself.

Although increased instability is likely, especially as the gross inequality of the current system leads to fragmentation within the elite itself, this does not in itself make socialism a likely outcome. This transformation to socialism can only come from the working class having a pre-existing organizational capacity to take advantage of these developments, especially in the most advanced countries, of which the United States is currently the most important. That capacity takes decades to build up and it's not a process that can be rushed or circumvented by some clever shortcuts and nor should it be.

It is always tempting to think that we are special, that ours is a special nation or a special generation, one that could accomplish gigantic feats. But sober analysis tells us that we are more likely to be an ordinary generation located in a dynamic but ultimately fairly ordinary time.

That isn't the end of the story however. Even if a successful insurrection is not on the horizon, it doesn't mean that we have no role to play. Our short-term tasks do not involve overthrowing capitalism — a mode of production cannot even be overthrown — but to construct the organizations that someday will outcompete it, organizations which can survive even if the upheavals do not come soon, even if no opportunities for transition appear for years. Should we survive even that bleak a scenario with an eco-system of institutions intact, the next generation of socialists can start from a much more advanced point.

There is much in this world that is outside our influence, at least at this juncture, but institution-building is not. But it won't be enough to try and persuade workers that a revolution or even socialism will solve their problems; rather we need to convince them that they have to do great things for the socialist organization, that the future itself depends on us all playing our role in that great collective project, outside of which there is no salvation.

Notes to Part Two

1. Restricting the franchise to workers, as the Russians did, is completely unworkable for the principle organ of democracy in modern society.
Likewise, the much vaunted unification of legislative and executive power is entirely counter-productive, draining the ability of the elected body
to freely criticize the executive committees which must appear.

Part Two: Movements for Change

The Battle Lines Are Drawn in the South:Right-Wing Neo-secessionism or a Third Reconstruction?

In this war for the heart and soul of the U.S., the battle for the South stands front and center.

By Bob Wing

DURHAM, North Carolina -- The heartless combination of the Supreme Court's gutting of the Voting Rights Act, the House Republicans flatly shunning the immigration bill, and the Trayvon Martin outrage should be a wake up call about the grave dangers posed by the far right and may give rise to a renewed motion among African-Americans that could give much needed new impetus and political focus to the progressive movement.

The negative policies and missteps of the Obama administration are often the target of progressive fire, and rightly so. But these take place in the context of (and are sometimes caused by) an extremely perilous development in U.S. politics: an alliance of energized right-wing populists with the most reactionary sector of Big Business has captured the Republican Party with "the unabashed ambition to reverse decades of economic and social policy by any means necessary." [1]

The GOP is in all-out nullificationist mode, rejecting any federal laws with which they disagree. They are using their power in the judiciary and Congress to block passage or implementation of anything they find distasteful at the federal level. And under the radar the Republicans are rapidly implementing a far flung right-wing program in the 28 states they currently control.

They have embarked on an unprecedented overhaul of government on behalf of the one percent and against all sectors of the poor and much of the working and middle classes, undermining the rights of all.

The main precedent in U.S. history for this kind of unbridled reactionary behavior was the states rights, pro-slavery position of the white South leading up to the Civil War. Dr. Martin Luther King, Jr. called out the attempts at nullification in his famous "I Have a Dream" speech and the movement of the sixties defeated it.

As shown in the ultra-conservative playground that is the North Carolina legislature, the new laws and structures of today's right-wing program are so extreme and in such stark contrast to the rest of the country that I believe both their strategy and their program should be called "Neo-Secession."

This nullification and neo-secession must be met by a renewed motion for freedom and social justice. The great scholar-activist Manning Marable, the leader of the powerful fightback in North Carolina NAACP President Rev. William Barber II, MSNBC's Melissa Harris-Perry, and others have called for a Third Reconstruction that builds on the post-Civil War first Reconstruction and the Civil Rights/Second Reconstruction. [2]

We are now at a pivotal point in this fight. The battle lines are drawn: Reactionary Nullification and Neo-Secession or Third Reconstruction?

Like the first secession, this second neo-secession is centered in the South even though it is a national movement with unusual strength in the upper Rocky Mountain and plains states in addition to the South. [3] Similarly racism, especially anti-Black racism, lies at its foundation even as the right-wing assaults all democratic, women's, immigrant and labor rights, social and environmental programs. Progressives in the South are rising to the challenge. But, deplorably, most Democrats, unions, progressives, and social justice forces barely have the South on their radar and rarely invest in it. This must change, and change rapidly.

A shift in progressive priorities and intensification of on-the-ground organizing are crucial to defeating the right's neo-secessionist agenda as well as to forge a sufficiently powerful "Third Reconstructionist" political force to successfully push back against the corporate leadership of the Democratic Party in the battles that must be waged against them along the way. We can righteously roast Obama all we want, but unless we can build a truly powerful force to his left that can simultaneously unite with moderates to break the political stranglehold of the far right, we will be spitting into the wind.

Neo-Secession and Third Reconstruction

Both the right-wing strategy of Nullification and Neo-Secession and the peoples fight for a Third Reconstruction are deeply rooted in U.S. history. Nullification was born in the nineteenth century as the slaveholders' legal theory that states have the right to ignore any federal legislation, judicial decision, or executive order that they disagree with. In practice it meant court decisions like Dred Scott, congressional filibusters, and reactionary legislation, and the consolidation of the slaveholders' power in the states. It was the prelude to Secession and Civil War.

Post Civil War, the victorious Union alliance with Blacks in the South then decreed Reconstruction, the most democratic, progressive, and racially just program in U.S. history up to that point.

New Reaction: From 1880s to the 1960s

By the 1880s, however, the Southern racists and their allies overthrew Reconstruction and set up another white supremacist regime characterized by legalized racial discrimination in all facets of life, the virtual reenslavement of Black labor, and a white monopoly on voting and political power. This regime even survived the New Deal and was not dismantled until the Civil Rights movement won passage of the Civil Rights Act in 1964 and the Voting Rights Act in 1965.

This Second Reconstruction not only finally ended the white dictatorship in the South but also ignited the anti-Vietnam War, Chicano, Asian American, Native American, women's, and gay rights movements. Together they gave rise to the War on Poverty and won unparalleled national rights and programs for workers, women, immigrants, the poor, and others.

Today the right wing is once again spewing out this racist legal theory of nullification and invoking a new civil war, hardly bloodless though not involving clashing armies, in an attempt to overthrow the Second Reconstruction. More important, they are putting it into practice at the federal, state, and local levels.

Due to decades of control of the presidency, they occupy most of the federal judiciary where they are systematically stripping away progressive laws, regulations, and rights -- even public education, the historic bedrock of the middle class. They control Congress through political hardball, gerrymandering and abuse of the rules. With control of two of the three branches of the federal government and the malevolent abuse of the filibuster and mass refusal of executive political appointments, they are strangling the Obama presidency. [4]

Meanwhile the Republicans control 28 states and numerous local jurisdictions in which they are moving to nullify federal legislation with which they disagree, qualitatively cut back on and privatize government and public education, drastically roll back the rights of people of color, women, workers, children, and gays and eliminate progressive income taxes in favor of regressive sales taxes. Lara M. Brown recently reminded us that "the vast majority of the laws under which each of us abide are state laws, not federal laws."

The recent Supreme Court decision invalidating the most powerful parts of the Voting Rights Act has opened the floodgates to voter suppression laws that heretofore have been ruled unconstitutional. Although there are still numerous Black legislators, David Bostis and Thomas Edsall assess that Republican gerrymandering, voter suppression, and Black legislators' loss of clout and committee chairs means that, "At the state level, Black voters and elected officials have less influence now than at any time since the civil rights era." [5]

Meanwhile the Great Recession has greatly increased already unacceptable levels of racial income and wealth inequality. The Trayvon Martin case traumatically revealed, once again, the grave dangers to Blacks living amidst white racism.

Red and Blue: the Modern Slave and Free

Outright secession would be political suicide since the right-wing led states clearly lack the power to win. But if they have their way the difference between Blue and Red states will soon be so stark as to be the modern analogue to the free and slave states or the legally segregated versus non-legally segregated states of the past.

This time the right wing wants it both ways: to benefit from staying in the Union yet at the same time to recreate numerous states in their own ideological image. This is why I think it is historically justifiable and politically useful to brand today's right wingers as nullificationist and neo-secessionist.

Nullification Returns

Nullification is one of the principal tactics of the right wing; neo-secession is its strategy and its program. Since the Nixon and especially the Reagan administrations, the right wing has sought to rout both the New Deal and the Civil Rights reconstruction, and replace it with an updated version of racism and reaction. The right reached both a new level of power and new level of extremism in reaction to the election of Barack Obama. It is our fight to defeat them and bring forth a new, Third Reconstruction that will make further strides toward ending racism and bringing justice for all.

Nothing Could be More
Neo-secessionist than North Carolina

North Carolina is a true purple state: Obama won the state in 2008 by less than one percent and lost it by two percent in 2012.

But through a combination of good luck and smart strategy, not to speak of state Democratic lethargy, Republican gerrymandering and the largesse of the right-wing retail mogul Art Pope, North Carolina has been the site of the Tea Party's most dramatic political victories and its most draconian legislative and social agenda. Pope's foundation finances 90 percent of the income of the state's leading right-wing groups. [6]

Yet, in 2012 the Republicans won the governorship and a majority in both houses of the legislature for the first time since the first Reconstruction. In fact they boast a supermajority in both houses. "Since then," says The New York Times, "the state government has become a demolition derby, tearing down years of progress in public education, tax policy, racial equality in the courtroom and access to the ballot."

In just its first two weeks the new legislature: (1) made North Carolina the only state to nullify all federally-mandated and funded extensions to unemployment, affecting 170,000 people. It also slashed the maximum unemployment benefit for new claims from $522 to $360 per week and the maximum length to 20 weeks. North Carolina has the fifth highest unemployment rate in the nation; (2) refused the federally-funded Medicare benefit that would have provided health care to an additional 500,000 North Carolinians; (3) moved to enshrine existing anti-union "right to work" laws in the state constitution; (4) passed voter ID laws, cutback early voting by half, and eliminated same-day registration; (5) legalized and subsidized fracking; and (6) passed a bill to purge state commissions and Superior Court judges they don't like.

Rev. Dr. William Barber II, the North Carolina State President of the NAACP and the main leader of the growing fightback, gives further details about what he calls the "vicious war on the poor":

"Piling further indignities on the poor, they also want to require people applying for temporary assistance or benefits to submit to criminal background checks, and force applicants to a job training program for low-income workers to take a drug test, for which they have to pay. Now the legislature wants to increase and expand taxes on groceries, haircuts and prescription drugs. They're even taking aim at poor children with a bill to increase the minimum income requirement for North Carolina's prekindergarten program, making it off limits to nearly 30,000 children who would have previously qualified. [7]

In addition, the legislature is moving to privatize Medicaid, slash public education funding to 2007 levels, end teacher tenure and place charter schools under separate governance; shut down most abortion clinics; and establish outlandish rules for ex-offenders to restore their voting rights.

This reactionary avalanche of neo-secession is being met by a burgeoning fightback. The North Carolina NAACP and the wide progressive coalition it has built called Historic Thousands on Jones Street (where the state capitol is located,) is fighting for what Rev. Barber enunciates as a Third Reconstruction.

This year they launched "Moral Monday": every Monday a demonstration against the legislature is followed by civil disobedience in the state house. In 11 such events so far, more than 700 people have been arrested, usually supported by thousands at the rallies. HKonJ and its member groups have flanked Moral Monday with a statewide and sectoral organizing campaign. [8]

Fighting Neo-Secession

The neo-secessionist strategy poses a highly complex set of challenges, distinct from a straight-up secession. The right must be defeated in public opinion, in the streets, in workplaces, and at the polls. And it must be defeated in numerous discrete congressional and legislative districts, as well as county and city races, governorships, legislatures, the Congress, and the presidency.

This will be protracted guerrilla political struggle. We must prepare ourselves to take advantage of big opportunities to mobilize the public and reshape public opinion when they are presented but also drill down into the electoral fights district by district. Only a gigantic and determined coalition of everyone who opposes the right can do this, not just in presidential elections but all levels of government.

However we also need a massive and well-organized progressive force to the left of Obama Democrats with a social justice left that can root this force among people of color, union, and other poor folk that can provide the backbone that the elite Democrats consistently show they lack. This is crucial not only to win all of these battles, but to make sure the right-wing program is eventually buried at every level and forever, and replaced by a Third Reconstruction.

This is not an ideological projection but a historically based reality of today's politics. I have detailed it, most recently; in "Can We Defeat the Racist Southern Strategy in 2012?" [9] Strikingly, African-American voters are dynamically growing and are the most progressive voting bloc in the country, and the even faster-growing Latino and Asian American populations are increasingly moving in the same direction. In 2012 Black voter participation exceeded that of all other groups. No other demographic group votes in such a unified liberal-progressive way.

Yet, it often appears that the leadership and membership of social justice nonprofits and progressive organizations, editorial boards, and actions are more racially segregated than the Fortune 500.

People of color are the anchor of what is now being called "the new majority" or the "rising American electorate" together with unmarried women, labor, and youth. Increased class gaps among seniors, married women, and the middle class also provide important organizing opportunities.

Of course the battle for a Third Reconstruction takes place in a vastly different global and national context than Reconstruction I and II. In this era of imperial decline, social austerity, and looming environmental catastrophe today's radical reconstruction would encompass not only the fight for racial justice but also intersect with labor battles and anti-cutback efforts, fights for immigrant, women's and LGBT rights, peace, and climate justice in new ways. Getting there will be complex but the potential exists for a social change movement in the U.S. that is both broader and more radical on a host of issues than previous progressive upsurges.

The Importance of the South

In this war for the heart and soul of the U.S., the battle for the South stands front and center.

Written off as redneck, ignorant Bible Belt country by too many liberals, the South is actually a heated center of battle against the right. Historically the defining feature of the South was the plantation economy and the racially-coerced labor that it was founded upon. However, plantations are now a thing of the past. Worldwide capitalist competition, technology, migration and immigration, gentrification/white flight and exurbs are transforming the Southern landscape, at different rates and in different ways. 10 Indeed Maryland and Virginia now rank in the top 10 in median household income while Southern states also occupy nine of the bottom [12].

The South (remember that both Texas and Florida were part of the Confederacy) has more population, more Black people, more poverty, more military installations, more congressional seats, and more electoral votes than any other region of the country, and it is growing. Despite right-to-work laws, it is also the only area besides California where union membership is growing.

The poison that lingers, however, is that Southern whites are far more conservative, Republican, and prone to white political solidarity than elsewhere. Nationally, anywhere between 55 percent and 60 percent of whites vote Republican in presidential elections. But Southern whites do so at a 70 percent-plus clip, rising to 90 percent in much of the Deep South in opposition to Obama. On the flip side there is a far greater percentage of African-American voters in the Southern states than elsewhere, topping at 35 percent in Mississippi. And like Blacks throughout the country, they consistently vote 90 percent Democratic. Black remigration to the South means that there is a higher percentage of African-Americans in that region than in many decades.

In fact the South has been wrongly stereotyped as a Republican monolith since the passage of the Civil Rights Act in 1964. Actually it was not until 1994 that the Republicans won a majority of the Southern congressional seats. There are way more African-American officeholders in the region than in any other part of the country. Democrats are generally stronger at the state and local levels than they are in presidential elections. New Deal and populist politics still exist among some working class whites and small farmers, and Latino and Asian immigration is growing.

No more 'Solid South'

Even in Mississippi the Republicans hold only a three-seat majority in the state's House. A proposed state constitutional amendment defining "personhood" as beginning at conception and prohibiting abortion "from the moment of fertilization" was defeated by 55 percent of voters in November 2011. And the longtime Black and human rights activist Chokwe Lumumba was just elected mayor of Jackson, the state's capital and largest city. [11] (Ed's note: Mayor Lumumba died while in office on February 25, 2014.)

Maryland long ago turned Blue, and Virginia and North Carolina are now true battleground states. After North Carolina, Georgia was the most competitive state won by Romney. And Texas and Mississippi are within shouting distance - and a lot of smart, hard work - of becoming battleground states. Progressive political forces and mass rumblings can be heard in every Southern state. This is where a broad coalition centered on African-Americans must be unleashed and the right wing routed in its own backyard.

The South is also the site of some of the most exciting social justice organizing in the country. [12]

The defeat of the Personhood amendment and the election of Chokwe Lumumba as mayor of Jackson highlight the growing power of groups like Mississippi One Voice, the Mississippi Black Leadership Summit and the Malcolm X Grassroots Movement in Mississippi.

'New Majority' Alliances

Virginia New Majority has burst on the scene with the state's most dynamic political field operation and as a key organizing force in the Virginia legislature. It may be the first social justice group to embark on an exciting new strategy of identifying, training, and fielding progressive candidates in key areas of the state. Florida New Majority has built one of the largest social justice electoral formations in the country as well as a potentially powerful alliance with the Service Employees International Union and other unions in this crucial battleground state. It is now making important new initiatives to develop its capacity to communicate regularly with the hundreds of thousands of people they meet at the doors as well with the organization of Freedom Clubs as a grassroots organization.

The battle for the South together with other purple and red states is once again likely to determine the future of this country. Next year's 50th Anniversary of the Freedom Summer provides an opportunity for people around the country to contribute to the battle in Mississippi and throughout the South.

The 50th Anniversary of the historic March on Washington will be marked by a landmark rally in Washington, DC on Aug. 28, 2013. Hopefully the anniversary will give breadth and depth to the emerging political motion ignited by the regressive Voting Rights Act decision and the Trayvon Martin travesty. The emergence of a renewed mass African-American-led grassroots motion would be a major step for the progressive movement as a whole as we take on the task of fighting to defeat neo-secession and forge a Third Reconstruction for jobs, peace and freedom.

Special thanks to my lifelong colleagues Max Elbaum and Linda Burn-

ham and to Jon Liss, Lynn Koh, Carl Davidson, Ajamu Dillahunt, Raymond Eurquhart, and Bill Fletcher Jr. for their comments, critiques, and suggestions.

[Bob Wing has been a social justice organizer and writer since 1968. He was the founding editor of ColorLines magazine and War Times newspaper. Bob lives in Durham, North Carolina, and can be contacted through Facebook.]

Footnotes:

1 Even the Brookings Institute centrist Thomas Mann and the American Enterprise Institute conservative Norman Ornstein are alarmed by what they call the Republican's "new nullification" strategy. They have devoted an entire book to this subject: It's Even Worse Than It Looks: How the American Constitutional System Collided with the New Politics of Extremism (2012).

2 Manning Marable, "The Third Reconstruction: Black Nationalism and Race in a Revolutionary America," Social Text, Autumn 1981. Reverend William Barber II: http://www.storyofamerica.org/reconstruction3. Melissa Harris-Perry: http://newsbusters.org/blogs/nathan-roush/2013/07/08/msnbc-harris-perry-claims-we-are-third-reconstruction-after-voting-rig .

3 Bruce Bartlett does a great job of tracing the origins of today's struggles to slavery days: http://www.thefiscaltimes.com/Columns/2012/05/04/Americas-Return-to-Political-Polarization.aspx#page1

4 In order to promote political stability, the framers of the U.S. Constitution created a unique fragmentation of the government into three branches (plus the Federal Reserve and the military) and a distinctively powerful division of power between the federal, state, county, and city jurisdictions. Combined with the decision to disperse and stagger elections, this system makes the governmental system of the U.S. uniquely stable. But, in an unintended consequence that Mann and Ornstein detail, it also makes it vulnerable to sabotage and nullification by a powerful political force like today's Republican Party which rejects the culture of compromise that is absolutely crucial to make tour very divided national governmental system work.

5 Bostis is quoted in Thomas Edsall, "The Decline of Black Power in the South," http://opinionator.blogs.nytimes.com/2013/07/10/the-decline-of-black-power-in-the-south/?emc=eta1 "

6 Much more on Pope at: http://www.southernstudies.org/person/art-pope

7 http://www.cnn.com/2013/05/29/opinion/barber-north-carolina-pro-test

8 A big question is how this increased street motion can not only be greatly increased but also translated into the electoral power necessary to strip away the Republican supermajorities and governorship in that state.

9 Bob Wing, "Can We Defeat the Racist Southern Strategy in 2012?" http://www.organizingupgrade.com/index.php/modules-menu/com-munity-organizing/item/728-can-we-defeat-the-racist-southern-strate-gy-in-2012

10 Bob Moser, now the executive editor of American Prospect magazine, advances an interesting and optimistic analysis of the political potential of the South in his 2008 book, Blue Dixie and in a recent special feature of American Prospect magazine entitled "The End of the Solid South" (http://prospect.org/article/end-solid-south).

11 Bob Wing, "From Mississippi Goddam to 'Jackson Hell Yes': Chokwe Lumumba is the New Mayor of Jackson": http://www.southernstudies.org/2013/06/voices-from-mississippi-goddam-to-jackson-hell-yes.html

12 There are many more important groups but the following are the social justice organizations with major civic engagement operations I am currently most knowledgeable about. Each of the groups I highlight is grounded in racial justice, new majority, and/or rising American elec-toral politics and strategies.

On 'LeftRoots': An Interview with Steve Williams

By Pat Fry and Anne Mitchell

Steve Williams co-founded People Organized to Win Employment Rights (POWER) and served as Executive Director for 14 years beginning in 1997. Upon leaving POWER, Steve co-authored with NTanya Lee an extensive report, "More Than We Imagined: Activists' Assessments on the Moment and the Way Forward" based on 9 months of interviews with 158 activists in 30 cities around the country, a project of Ear to the Ground. Currently, Steve is a leader of a new organization – LeftRoots. On February 16, 2014, Steve was presented with the Louis E. Burnham Fund award for outstanding activism at a program held at the Schomburg Center for Research in Black Culture in Harlem. Before the award program, on Feb, 16, 2014, Anne Mitchell and Pat Fry interviewed Steve for Dialogue & Initiative.

What were the key experiences and lessons you took from your 14 years as Executive Director of POWER?

We started POWER in 1997 right in the aftermath of Bill Clinton and the Republicans joining together to sign the Welfare Reform legislation. That particular experience of having a cabal of millionaires making decisions over the lives of millions of low income people was really informative. Much of the rhetoric and debate that was happening around that legislation centered on this idea that in the context of poverty, poor people were the problem. It wasn't structural issues with the economy. It wasn't the history of bad politics. It wasn't inequitable distribution of resources. It was poor people who were the problem.

One of the two main headings of the legislation was "Personal Responsibility." It seemed to us in starting POWER that this was going to be the context and would continue to be the case until people who are most directly impacted by welfare and poverty issues had an opportunity to come together, analyze the situation and take collective action. That's what we were trying to do with POWER – create a space for low-income, working class folks to be able to engage in the public policy debates that impact their lives.

We also saw at the time the transformations that were happening in the global capitalist system where maybe 50 years ago, the folks who were now receiving public assistance and doing workfare in San Francisco, if they had lived in Detroit or some other industrialized area, regardless of whether or not they had graduated from high school or gone to college, would have been able to get a job that paid wages sufficient to take care of their families and live a relatively decent life.

The transformations in capitalism meant that this opportunity no longer existed. More and more people were being thrown out into the periphery of the capitalist system and our analysis was that welfare recipients were essentially in the vanguard of that but that other sectors of the working class in the U.S. and around the world were going to be thrown out as well. We wanted to develop a model whereby we were organizing low income folks to not only deal with immediate issues that were impacting their lives but also develop the consciousness to then be able to take on globalized systems of capitalism, white supremacy and patriarchy.

In 15 years of POWER, the thing that constantly inspired and generated more and more momentum for the work was the fact that there was a real hunger for that. Over time at POWER we developed a leadership and political education program that we called POWER University. A lot of folks said we were essentially wasting time and that if members had 10 hours a week to devote to work with POWER, that the work should be devoted to developing press releases, and doing outreach. People said it was a waste of time to step back and assess conditions that were going on around us, draw out the lessons from our campaign experience and other movement experience. Our experience was exactly the opposite. In fact, the more people participated in the political education and leadership development program, the more time they committed to the organization. They had more capacity to take up roles that someone just walking in off the street probably wouldn't have been in a position to take up.

In my mind, trying to figure out this intersection between practice of engaging in collective struggle, but also trying to figure out the spaces whereby people are developing new capacities is a critical ingredient of what it means to do social movement organizing work.

There is a good deal of grass roots organizing work going on today. Do you see the same attention to education and training taking place in other campaigns and organizations?

No. I think it is exciting that there are new developments beginning to take root. You have networks of organizations like the Right to the City, or Grassroots Global Justice or National People's Action that recently went through an interesting member-driven political education process, but I think that a lot of that is new and is growing out of the complexity of the conditions that we are in right now. So a lot of organizations are realizing that the tactics that they were engaging in for a long time are not as effective and that we are still getting our asses handed to us. In order for us to make real progress means that we are going to have to do our work differently and we are going to have to understand better what it is that we are up against.

I do think that there is an interesting push right now with new leadership development and political education programs emerging out of a lot of organizations. But I think some of the challenge is that there are very few spaces for the trainers and the organizers to actually develop their world view.

For me, I was incredibly fortunate soon after starting POWER to have the chance to go to South Africa to participate in the South African Communist Party congress. That completely blew my mind and reshaped what it is that I thought was necessary and what I thought was possible working with working class folks.

I remember seeing 900 Black South Africans debating the future of their country, talking about what role the public sector would play in the expansion of the economy and having high level conversations. They would have debate and deliberations for two or two and half hours and then they would take a break. Somebody would stand up and they would start singing freedom songs and toy toy for 15 minutes.

After one of these breaks, I walked out to a local bookstore that had set up a little stand and while looking at the books this guy comes walking up behind me and says, "Well, you have to understand that when Marx wrote the Poverty of Philosophy, he was writing in response to Hegel who wrote the Philosophy of Poverty, and so you have to put this in context." I said, "oh, well, hi, my name is Steve. So what do you do? You must be a professor somewhere. And he said, "no, no, I am a diamond miner." I said, "oh you used to be a diamond miner but then you went to the university and now you are a professor." He said, "no, no, I am still a diamond miner. I am a shop steward for my union and one of the processes in the anti-apartheid struggle was that all the shop stewards wound up having two weeks of political education run by the SACP."

I was still at the point where I was kicking and screaming not wanting to read all the dead white men. Here I am being schooled by a diamond miner who not only engaged in that process of reading this hard theoretical text, not in his first language, but also talked very specifically about the role that that played in sharpening his capacity to play a leadership role in the broader social movement.

One of the challenges that we are dealing with in the United States is that although there are increasing outlets for popular education and political education, it's not necessarily grounded in an ideological tradition or in the long trajectory of social movements. People are doing an incredibly organic job of piecing stuff together, but we are never going to be able to advance the ball down the field if we are constantly reinventing the wheel. We have to take advantage of the work that other organizers and activists have done before us.

I think that in some respects it is a generational split. I wound up being at the older edge of the constellation of organizers and activists that I interact with. There are certainly some older folks but for the most part people are in their 20s and 30s and most of those folks were politicized after the fall of the Soviet Union and at a time when left organizations in the United States did not have as broad an influence as they did in the 1960s and 70s.

A lot of folks in my generation who I think have a radical world view and have revolutionary inclinations don't have any space to hone that. People oftentimes become involved in social movement work and see that as an outlet for their political activity. Part of what has happened over the last 10 or 15 years is that people have realized that we continue to suffer major defeats but it's not a question of us not working hard enough. The equation can't be that whatever the gap is between where we are now and where we want to go, simply being us working harder. There has to be something that is done qualitatively different but people don't know exactly what that is. I think that the political education that is emerging out of organizations now is pointing in the right direction but it is not necessarily grounded in the lessons of past social movements, both in this country and around the world.

When were you in South Africa for the SACP Congress?

It was 1998. I was in Cuba in 1997. They were two pivotal moments for me in developing as a leftist. It was having lived in the context of Reagan and Thatcher's insistence that there is no alternative to capitalism and then seeing a living example of it in Cuba, and how in a lot of respects it seemed way more attractive than what I saw in the United States. And then going to South Africa the year after and seeing what a vibrant social movement looks like were for me two pivotal pieces that have then really shaped a lot of the work that we have been doing at POWER and that I have been doing since.

What led you to undertake the "Ear to the Ground" interview project?

It was a real hunger to be able to build a multi-sectoral effective social movement and constantly experiencing challenges and difficulties in doing that. I remember in 2008 with the economic bubble bursting, I often thought that the left doesn't pay significant enough attention to the economy. We often pay a lot of attention to the role of the state, the actions of the state but not as much attention, I think, to the economic base. Obviously, with the economic crisis it seemed that the particular fissures that existed within the capitalist system were starting to break and the left wasn't really positioned to be able to speak to that. One of our big slogans was "bail out the people not the banks" which seems like an important and helpful impulse but it also seemed to ignore the fact that there was an actual crisis.

We weren't able to speak to broad demands, for example, like nationalizing the banks. You had mainstream economists like Paul Krugman and Joseph Stiglitz talking about the need to nationalize the banks and the left wasn't talking about that.

Within POWER we developed political education curriculum to deepen our understanding of what was going on and the framing was that this was a crisis of the capitalist system. We remember at the time the corporate media talking about it as a problem of greed, of greedy investment bankers and Bernie Madoff but the system was fine.

We were arguing that this is a problem of capitalism. And we ran that with the members and I fully anticipated that that was going to be a controversial point that we would spend the rest of the session talking through those dynamics. The first person raised her hand and she said, "ok, I get what you are saying that the capitalist system is always going to be against the interests of working class people, and people around the globe. I get that, but what's the alternative?"

It was a breakthrough for me to see how clearly people see capitalism as the enemy. People don't see it as the vehicle that is going to lead to liberation and prosperity. But on the flip side people are also very clear that they don't know that there is another alternative. I think that binds people's ability and willingness to step out and take risks. I didn't feel prepared to lead some of that discussion about, what is the alternative? I think oftentimes we do these hyper fantastic utopian exercises about what we want the world to look like but we need to be able to talk about a system, a new social structure that allows all of those positive by-products to come into being.

I decided to leave POWER in large part to be able to answer the question, are social movements in a place where we really want to have that level of conversation? Already I had been thinking about the need for us to engage in a process of developing cadre amongst folks who are already deeply rooted in key sectors of the working class. I didn't know how other people were reading this particular moment, so I decided to leave and build on some of my reading of Amilcar Cabral's experience in Guinea Bissau. Cabral talked about his experience returning home after being trained as a student in Portugal which was funded by the Portuguese government to walk around as an agronomist and talk to the people of Cape Verde and Guinea Bissau. He attributed that experience as a key moment where he had the opportunity to develop a much sharper and grounded view of what was happening in his country.

Talk to people, figure out what are their hopes, dreams, and aspirations – what are they pissed off about? We didn't take on a project that ambitious but we decided to focus on organizers and activists who are engaged in social movements and see what those folks were thinking across the country. We started in March of 2012. It was this really interesting moment, right after the last of the Occupy encampments had been broken up. It was still fresh on the heels of the mobilizations that had happened throughout North Africa, in the Middle East, the Arab Spring, Wisconsin, so in some really important ways a lot of the paradigms about how grass roots and community and labor organizing was happening in the United States had been broken up. It was this incredible opportunity to go around and talk to other organizers and activists about what they were seeing, what they wanted, and how it is that they thought their work was contributing to that.

Talk about the model of "Transformative Organizing." Does this model speak to some of the limitations that you talked about? How do you define this method of organizing?

With transformative organizing, we are trying to touch on three main points. The first goes back to some basic precepts of organizing. In order to be able to make fundamental social change we have to build up the organizational capacity of the disposed to be able to take collective action. There are going to be a lot of different facets to that fight – communications, legislative, lobbying.

In some ways the idea of organizing has really gotten downplayed in the movement broadly and in the left. We really want to come back to this fundamental idea of the need to build organization. It's also rooted in the idea that organizations aren't just instruments to be used in effecting change but ultimately, that by participating in a collective project with other people, we are all transformed in that process. It's where this notion of transformation comes from. It's not just that organizations are important because they allow us the mechanism to be able to exert collective power. Organizations are also important because we develop skills of solidarity by developing relationships and in that process we change who we are.

Going back to the experience in Cape Verde and Guinea Bissau, Cabral - and other revolutionaries have talked about this as well – put forward the idea that revolution as an insurrectional single moment has historically not been proved to be an effective framework. To effect revolutionary change, not only requires the ability to achieve state power. Some people have done that through violent means in various countries, and some folks like in Venezuela or Bolivia have been able to do that through electoral channels.

That's not the end of the game. There is still the process of developing popular capacity, developing protagonism where people see themselves as the drivers of history and are then able and willing to step into leadership roles in society, whether it is running school boards, or worker co-ops, etc. Developing that capacity is important and organization can be a critical laboratory for people to develop their skills.

The transformational aspect of organization is just as important as the effective social change aspect of organizations. Ultimately, all of our organizing work has to be driven by a guiding vision of the fundamental social transformation that we want to make. A part of that is developing capacity of leaders but that can't be the extent of what it is that we are doing.

In the same way we are trying to effect reforms and build institutions that help meet people's basic needs and increase their capacity to be able to fight but we are not going to sacrifice our long term objective of building people's power for the sake of winning a short term reform fight. The transformative organizing model is very much about trying to consciously situate itself within a guiding vision of what's the fundamental social transformation that we want and we recognize that that vision will likely evolve over the course of our engaging in campaign fights, developing new relationships with people inside of our organizations and allied relationships with other organizations in this country and around the world.

That vision will change but the organization's work is constantly informed and fed by this larger vision. Those are three of the key principles that we are trying to advance with this notion of transformative organizing.

What are some of the lessons you have learned in building multi-racial organization?

POWER is a multi-racial organization, mostly African American and Latino but there are also some white working class folks. In the early history of the organization much of our line was essentially the Rodney King line, "can't we just all get along?" We pushed a little bit beyond that to say "we are all in the same boat" but the lived reality of folks is radically different. People didn't see that we are all in the same boat. African American folks were dealing with a very particular set of issues such as unemployment, being completely dislocated from the formal workforce, the rise of the prison-industrial complex. Latinos were dealing with immigration raids and attacks as well as hyper-exploitation in jobs.

Latinos could get jobs but they wouldn't always get paid for the jobs that they got and when they did get paid they often are paid less than minimum wage or really low wage. Nevertheless they could actually get jobs. The Latino members would look at the African American members and think, "well you must be lazy because I can get a job anywhere." In reality, African Americans are looking for a job but get turned away and they know that many of the jobs that the Latinos are getting in San Francisco are jobs that their parents or grandparents once did as unionized employees. So African Americans see Latino immigrants as the folks who have "stolen their jobs." In my mind, the line that we were taking organizationally was insufficient for the very real experiences that people were having.

It wasn't until the racial relationships within the organization came to a head that we were pushed to try to figure out a different way of addressing the problem. It was only in our willingness to talk explicitly about imperialism that we found the common root in each others' experiences. It wasn't until we went deep beneath the surface to talk about that lived historical reality and walk each group through it that then people were like, "oh, I get it now." And then you had an inseparable bond but it meant that we had to be willing to talk about imperialism with the members and we were scared to do it at first. We were a small organization but we made the decision to talk about it and when we did, we found that the unity coming out of that process was way more genuine and sincere. We actually made a qualitative leap in solidarity.

When you talk about imperialism being a key understanding, do you mean, for example, how NAFTA is forcing immigrants out of their homelands?

It included that but we were also talking about centuries-old processes. We essentially looked at the experience of African Americans and Latinos in relationship to the United States. We went all the way back to the transatlantic slave trade and talked about slavery, looked at Reconstruction and the period from Reconstruction to the Civil Rights movement and then the contemporary state of Black America. Some of the aspects of that were economic but some of it was cultural. We used a couple of clips from Roots and one of them was where Kunta Kinte is getting whipped and his master is trying to get him to adopt the name Toby. People had already seen how Africans' language was stripped from them and then they saw this process of people having new names imposed upon them. It was interesting because then a lot of the Latinos ended up saying "My name is Juanita but a lot of white people in San Francisco can't pronounce that so then they decide to call me June, or whatever. I would tell them my name is not June. My name is Juanita. You need to learn how to pronounce it."

In California, the fight around multi-culturalism and the right to speak Spanish in public settings is still a very live memory for folks. So when Latinos learned about African immigrants' languages being stripped from them, it resonated. On the flip side we ended up looking at the historic westward expansion of the United States and talked about California's history as part of Mexico until it was stolen by the United States. We then looked at the Civil War period when the Southern slave states were proposing to annex Central America, particularly Nicaragua, to make it a slave state. In the context of the Civil War we were able to make the Black-Brown connection that virtually no one in the room had known anything about.

Then, we fast forwarded and looked at the history of the Sandinista Nicaraguan revolution, the role that the United States played in undermining it and then we looked at NAFTA and the contemporary situation. We posed to people the question, what are the similarities and what are the differences that you see? To a person, people said, "look there are some differences that we are experiencing today but they are differences that trace back to a similar historical dynamic. All of us have had our language, our names, our cultures, and our histories stripped from us." It was only in being willing to talk about that particular history that opened up the understanding that if imperialism is a part of an expansionist aspect of capitalism and that's what capitalism is, we share a common history of exploitation and oppression. That system is not going to carry us to liberation.

The organization and the movement has to be willing to engage in that conversation which then means that the politics of the organization can't be trying to develop a New Deal version of capitalism. Our alternative can't be Keynesian capitalism because we are still playing out the same dynamics. In that way, our members started to see that this is all connected and we have reason to be together in an organization. Even though it is difficult and clunky, the political objective is what makes that work.

Talk about your most recent project, LeftRoots. How do you see building LeftRoots and what do you see for its future?

A lot of the motivation behind LeftRoots goes back to what I was talking about before. Folks who are engaged in community, labor, and grassroots organizing are committed to changing the world in an era when the Left has been largely marginalized. For some legitimate and some not so legitimate reasons a lot of younger organizers and activists have either consciously or unconsciously made the decision not to join up with revolutionary left organizations. This has stunted our collective political development.

On the flip side, I think the left that exists in the United States right now is too disconnected from the social sectors that have a material interest in toppling capitalism, white supremacy and patriarchy. Most left communist events are mainly older, white, middle class men. I think they have an important role to play in building a movement toward liberation but they can't be the majority or the center of that particular movement.

Interestingly enough, a lot of these organizers, whether in the trade union movement or community organizations, have over the last decade or decade and a half developed really strong organic relationships with rank and file leaders in our communities or workplaces or schools. They have developed trust and have cultivated capacities to such an extent that I think people are outgrowing their organizations. A lot of organizations, because of the way they are funded, are located in a particular issue, or specific geographic area and we have had difficulty in moments like the economic crisis of actually building multi-sectoral organizing.

LeftRoots is a space designed to try to develop cadre amongst left-ists who are engaged in social movement work. We see ourselves distinct from most social movement organizations because we are solidly situated around an explicit assessment of capitalism, white supremacy and patriarchy. We are talking about the need for 21st century socialism.

We are different from most left organizations because we are not arguing for one particular trend or one particular ideological point of view. We think that within LeftRoots there will likely be multiple tendencies and views. We think that by developing our strategic lit-eracy and being able to better argue how it is that the work that we are doing right now will lead us towards developing a movement for liberation.

If people can articulate that strategic orientation more sharply, it means that the movement is going to be in a better place. From there, hopefully, there will be more and more opportunity for left organiza-tions to come into existence. Similar to what happened in Latin Amer-ica, we think that if there are new cadre that emerge out of social movements, that it will essentially create a momentum that changes the way that left organizations function in the United States and that change the way social movements function in the United States. In some ways, the strengths of both will compliment the weaknesses of the other.

LeftRoots is intending to create that space nationally for social move-ment leftists in the United States. We started out by developing a mem-bership branch in the Bay Area. We currently have 50 folks and later this year we are planning on expanding out to other parts of the country. In the meantime, we are sponsoring both online and in-person discus-sions with social movement leftists so that people have the opportunity to develop relationships, gain more familiarity with the work and the insights growing out of that work. Our hope is that we will be able to cohere a group of folks so that when moments like Occupy jumps off again, we have the trust, the relationships and the capacity to be able to identify opportunities to intervene and move our respective bases to then take advantage of the weaknesses, the vulnerabilities that capital is experiencing.

If someone wants to get in touch with LeftRoots and be a part of it, what do they do?

We will have a website soon: LeftRoots.net. In the meantime, people can email, info@LeftRoots.net and get in touch with us.

Are you in touch with people around the country to duplicate what you are building in the Bay Area?

We started in April last year hosting what we call "hangouts" – online gatherings for social movement leftists to begin a series of conversations with one another. The first hangout NTanya and I discussed our findings from the Ear to the Ground project. For the second one, Marta Harnecker, the Chilean political scientist discussed the emergence of social movement leftists in Latin America. We distributed an article that she wrote and asked people to read it and then hosted the hangout where we interviewed Marta. People were able to pose questions to Marta and to other participants in the hangout. It's an attempt to begin building relationships with one another.
We now have had four or five hangouts. We are trying to do them every other month. We have found a platform that seems to work relatively well right now so a lot of the bumps and hurdles we experienced have been worked through.

We were initially anticipating getting 50 to 75 folks on these hangouts and we wound up getting anywhere from 120 to 200 people. Just as exciting, people in their communities ended up organizing local reading groups around the articles and then participated. So there has actually been a lot more excitement and enthusiasm about LeftRoots as a project than what we had initially anticipated.

That is going to be continuing. One of the first projects that the Bay Area branch of LeftRoots is taking up is developing a strategy commission where we are going to try to engage in a series of discussions and research projects to assess present day conditions, our vision of liberation and then begin projecting different strategic orientations.

We want to have those conversations with folks around the country. Part of what we are finding is that there are other groupings like LeftRoots in cities across the country. For us, we don't necessarily want or feel the need for everybody to get involved in LeftRoots. We want to have a movement-wide conversation with organizations that already exist and where organizations do not exist, we are excited about helping to get those off the ground.

How do you see LeftRoots engaging in struggles for economic justice, jobs, homelessness, in the day to day?

The reality is that a large number of members in LeftRoots are engaged in those fights. LeftRoots sees itself as providing support to strengthen those fights that are already taking place. LeftRoots is not looking to duplicate efforts that already exist but instead arm organizers and leaders in those particular struggles with the tools necessary to be able to engage in those fights more effectively.

We want to develop relationships with organizers and activists and leaders in other fights. We might be willing to provide support at key moments in those struggles. That is the first and the primary. But when there are opportunities where none of our particular organizations are engaging in those particular fights then LeftRoots would want to be able to intervene. It creates an opportunity for us to engage in collective activity and gives us more opportunity to develop new skills and evaluate lessons. It also begins to develop a new model of what it looks like to engage in some of our social movement fights.

One example that we have been thinking about in the Bay Area is the dynamic that just played out with the BART (Bay Area Rapid Transit) strike. The unions focused on health and safety conditions. In the meantime, the corporate media was portraying the BART workers as inconsiderate, privileged workers who got paid more than anybody else and they should be thankful to have a job. The union was never really able to overcome that particular framing. In our mind, it is an interesting contrast to the how the Chicago Teachers Union framed their fight. Their fight was about job security and wages but it was also very much about quality education for all students in the Chicago public school system.

The BART workers unions didn't take up that particular framing. POWER has been doing a lot of transit justice work so we had hoped that they would have reached out to us. In my mind, it would have been a very interesting experiment if the BART workers union, in addition to trying to increase the wages and improve the health and safety protections for the workers had talked about the need to lower the cost of BART so that it serves workers who work late nights and weekends. And had the unions connected its demands to disarming the BART police officers who have a long history of using unauthorized force to kill young people like Oscar Grant or homeless people. There are particular ways in which their demands could have been framed more broadly. We hope LeftRoots is able to step into spaces and assert that broader demands for quality public transportation throughout the Bay Area. That's the way we have been thinking about our connection to economic justice.

What's the average age of LeftRoots members?

My guess is 33. I'm 44 and I believe that I am the fourth oldest. There are two older activists who were active with the new communist movement in the 1970s and 80s. Everybody else was born at least in the late 1960s and most folks in the 1980s.

On the demographics, it is a model of trying to re-shift the composi-tion of the left in a number of ways. Our members are about 85 percent People of Color and 70 percent women or transgender folks. There are rank and file members of community organizations such as POWER.

Most folks would not identify our members as typical people from the left. In addition to developing skills we are trying to get people to think about the left, to think about socialists in a way that is very much rooted in the dreams and aspirations of people who have been historically op-pressed and exploited by the system of capitalism.

An Autumn Convergence for Peace, Justice and Ecological Survival

By Mark Solomon

Progressive organizations across the country have become increasingly motivated to address the need for greater unity, focus and cohesion among disparate groups. A sense of urgency is driven by a growing awareness that the diffusion of organizational energy into scores of unconnected single issue groups and campaigns, while each vitally needed, undermines the strength and political coherence of the battle to defeat the right and to set the country on an irreversible road to progress and heightened democracy.

In efforts to forge cooperation among peace, justice and environmental organizations in particular, there has been no intent to divert any of them from their specific agendas and priorities. Rather, the objective of fostering a convergence has been to build cooperation and mutual support across organizational lines aimed at strengthening critical battles on pressing issues. That process involves building stronger and more unified campaigns while erecting a coherent progressive program to effectively engage and mobilize a broader public. At its root, momentum for converging organizations, movements and campaigns is anchored on an awareness of the inseparable nature of the struggles borne by progressives. There is an indisputable interdependence between ending a militarized economy, creating jobs built upon a Green New Deal and overcoming the growing environmental crisis.

Those pressing concerns have led to gatherings around the country to foster such a convergence. Conferences and actions aimed at movement cooperation have recently taken place from Arizona to Massachusetts. An Earth Day convergence called for May 1, 2014 embraces a call for peace, justice, jobs and human rights as an indispensable aspect of building a united movement for environmental survival. A national LeftRoots project, anchored largely on the leadership of oppressed nationalities, is aimed at building substantive unity on the left.

In Greater Boston, the search for movement unity and cooperation has been going on for nearly six years beginning with the formation in 2008 of the Majority Agenda Project, an effort by a group of activists, including CCDS members, to build a unified movement across lines that separated the antiwar, economic justice and environmental movements. That effort culminated in the hugely successful "Budget for All" resolution that attained ballot placement in about 40% of the state's legislative districts in the 2012 election. Combining demands to stop the budget cuts, invest in vast job programs, tax the rich and end the wars, the Budget for All campaign brought together a powerful coalition of peace, community, civil and human rights, labor and religious organizations that won support of around 70% of voters - including majorities in predominantly Republican areas.

'Budget for All' Gives Focus

The Budget for All campaign provided a stimulus for the organization of an "Autumn Convergence" in November 2013 of activists from initiating groups such as Massachusetts Peace Action, American Friends Service Committee, Women's International League for Peace and Freedom, Massachusetts Global Action/Encuentro 5 and others. While the more than 120 participants tended to be older and whiter, a significant number of younger people and people of color joined the effort to seek common ground and collaboration among progressive activists.

Mixing traditional and innovative elements, the conference opened with a panel discussion on movement building with speakers from the labor, environmental and antiwar movements who articulated the concerns of their respective constituencies. (CCDS' former co-chair Leslie Cagan represented the antiwar movement.) The panel was followed by an innovative effort to spark discussion among activists from different movements. Participants were given numbers that directed them to tables arranged to seat ten people heretofore generally unknown to each other. Participants engaged in energetic discussion of barriers to be overcome in building mutual support among different movement sectors while exploring the pressing issues that mandate cooperation. (Post-conference evaluations identified those discussions as one of the most rewarding aspects of the convergence.)

The next phase of the convergence was the convening of seven workshops. Among them, four agreed to continue working beyond the autumn gathering. A workshop on formulating an overarching vision for the convergence is continuing its effort "to advance a vision of a humane and just society...seeking to express in clear and accessible language the values of equality, democracy, community and fellowship that the [envisioned] society would encompass."

A workshop on developing an inclusive public policy agenda is working on implementation of the aforementioned-shared vision. A policy draft has outlined a compressive program touching upon every major need - projecting an integration of peace, social and economic justice and environmental survival movements, thus offering clear solutions to the crises now engulfing our society. That policy agenda, when completed, will embrace the widest range of issues, focusing sharply upon struggle against inequality, racism, sexism and homophobia and charting a path to a heightened democracy in the workplace, the financial system and the political arena.

A workshop on connecting with other convergence efforts at home and abroad is aimed at building the broadest possible alliances heading toward the United States Social Forum in 2015.

A workshop on conversion and jobs is focused upon the Massachusetts economy that is heavily invested in unsustainable military research and weapons production. The workshop has developed a concrete plan to build actions aimed at moving the state from military spending and fossil fuels to green jobs and extensive programs to upgrade and transform the state's aging infrastructure. Calling for a new economy for Massachusetts, the workshop is looking toward attaining Pentagon transition funds (a little known Pentagon program) to develop green energy and conversion of a local coal-fired plant to green manufacturing (possible wind turbines). The workshop is developing legislation for creation of a Massachusetts "green futures" commission and is organizing a series of forums on economic transition from a militarized economy to a green economy.

Coalescing the interests and energies of peace, jobs and ecology movements, the conversion workshop and all the continuing workshops are confirming the value and potential of the Autumn Convergence. The organizing committee continues to meet, energized by a strong desire of many participants to move forward together in continuing to unite the disparate strands of the progressive movement. It is developing tools to enable the Convergence participants to stay in touch while reaching out to activists who were not part of the November 2013 event. A follow-up spring-summer Convergence is in the works aimed at strengthening the actions that cut across various groups, causes and communities. Those are the threads that bring the diverse sectors of the movement together. Convergence is about making those threads visible, irreversible and ultimately victorious.

To Make a Great Salad,
The Field Must First be Tilled:
Toward the Implementation of
21st Century Democracy and Socialism

*[William Lloyd Garrison's] career...
exemplifies the fault line that in
democratic politics separates the
insiders, who think progress comes
from quiet lobbying with the halls of
power, from the outsiders, who insist
that only public manifestations of
dissatisfaction can overcome institutional inertia" (Mayer, 1998, p. xiv).*

*"We have to understand that building a
political force cannot be built without
building a social force. The strength
of the organization should be assessed not so much by the number of
members it has...but by the influence it has in society...Member identity
ought to be legitimized by what is done outside not inside the party"
(Harnecker, 2007, pp. 83-84).*

By Jay D. Jurie

Lessons from the values, principles and goals of 21st Century Socialism can be combined with our own history in the U.S. In brief, through
a greater replacement of the ownership of the state with more direct
forms of popular ownership and social control, the new 21st Century
Socialist approach stands in contrast with older conceptions and forms
of socialism. Although there have been some shifts in orientation since
this approach was first articulated, its underlying constructs have remained relatively constant.

Although all forms of socialism would replace a capitalist elite and seek
an end to economic exploitation, 21st Century Socialism relies more
heavily on forms of workplace and participatory democracy rather than
on a state socialist party or a state bureaucracy, and among other con-

siderations, expands usage of electronic technology to enhance democratic participation as well as to manage the economy (Dieterich, 2007; Moulian, 2000). One leading example, that of the Venezuelan Bolivarian Revolution involves something of a three-tiered arrangement: a foundational emphasis on the social ownership of the means of production, worker decision-making with regard to production, and the primacy of communal needs in the setting of worker decision-making priorities (Harnecker, 2010; Lebowitz, 2014).

Strategizing the implementation of such considerations are key to effecting a transition to 21st Century Socialism. Whereas some may perceive a desirable future society can be achieved "by any means necessary," it's increasingly understood the means are integral to, and must be consonant with, the ends. In the U.S., there's been comparatively little discussion of the means by which several Latin American models pursuing versions of 21st Century Socialism have come to power and set the stage for further change.

In all instances thus far it's readily apparent an electoral strategy has been pursued. After a failed coup, Hugo Chavez and the Bolivarian Movement of Venezuela, similar to Salvador Allende's Popular Unity government in Chile during the early 1970s, followed an electoral path to power (Clark & Grove, 2013; Petras, 2008; Press TV, 2012, Quinones, 2014). Of course, elections are both preceded by and accompanied with, a great deal of organizing, agitation, various types of public engagement, publicity, and so on. They represent a culmination of a massive effort to reframe not only the nature of the state, but to mobilize and reconfigure the underpinnings of the economy and civil society (Harnecker, 2005; Petras, 1969).

Electoral Effort Needs Interaction with Mass Base

From these examples, it is evident that a successful electoral effort must bear a reflexive relation with a mass base sufficient to win elections. In turn, electoral victories must serve to enlarge, sustain, and empower that bloc through the prospect of future gains and victories, electoral and non-electoral alike. In this sense are "outside" and "inside" linked to the overall strategy of not just gains at the polls, but more profound social transformation. This aspect alone presents a problem in the U.S. where the expectation is that once election day has come and gone, people stay uninvolved until the next elections roll along.

An "inside" strategy can have several meanings, including work carried out strictly within one political party, or within the electoral framework, or most broadly, through various existing institutional channels of society. In the U.S., participation within the Democratic Party has come to represent what's mostly meant by inside work, and this has most con- spicuously taken the form of realignment. Classically, realignment is a gradualist approach reliant upon transforming the Democratic Party from the inside, compelling it to adopt policy priorities that are more progressive. Progressive Democrats of America provides one exam- ple:

"We are a grassroots PAC operating inside the Democratic Party, and outside in movements for peace and justice. Our inside/outside strategy is guided by the belief that a lasting majority will require a revitalized Democratic Party built on firm progressive principles" (2013).

Leaving apart the question of whether a grassroots PAC can gain suf- ficient mass or resources to produce the desired effect on the Demo- cratic Party, what is typically of greater relevance when considering this definition of realignment is the apparent absence of any strategy whereby that might take place. One way to consider the question is to ask how, exactly, does outside work contribute to internal Party change? It would seem that what is to be gained, and how, is rarely considered. Does realignment only mean influencing existing office- holders or candidates to adopt more progressive conditions, or is there an implicit expectation that eventually candidates from the ranks of ex- plicitly progressive organizations would run as Democrats with some chance of winning?

In practical terms, these are questions that can only be answered accord- ing to situational context, and then only predicated upon an assessment of the strength and sophistication of the electoral base. To the extent a local-level realignment strategy is successful, it must open the door to wider inside initiatives that may well transcend the boundaries of the Democratic Party. For it to be successful, it must be audacious, it must advance a more pro-active radical agenda. It must seek to capture the dialog, if not to actually seize control of the local Party.

Advocates of realignment have been far too timid for far too long, in- vesting precious time and energy following bland, mainstream, pro-cor- porate candidates with only vestigial ties to progressive cultural issues and superficial interest in economic justice and democracy, in the hopes that would somehow build a progressive majority.

While conventional wisdom tells us a weaker base compels greater con- ventional reliance on existing, more centrist politicians, what it also means is an even greater need for radicals to challenge the status quo. Where a stronger foundation has been laid, perhaps after a considerable period of agitation, it eventually becomes more feasible for progressive organizations to run candidates under their own banner.

Development of a progressive base outside the electoral arena is absolutely imperative. Most essentially, what work outside the limits of the electoral arena must do is re-frame, or shape, the public debate, which in turn will inform the struggle inside mainstream political parties. Only larger, more significant issues can perform this function. History and an examination of current conditions, along with "actually existing" 21st Century Socialism, reveals both the need for, and significance, of well-focused and well-developed outside organizing.

In the case of the U.S., the abolition movement of the mid-19th Century was unsuccessful at electing its own members, but had a profound influence on the national agenda that swayed electoral outcomes (Mayer, 1998). In Venezuela, economic and social inequities, spurred in part by political corruption and repression, produced a constitutional crisis that ultimately led to the election of Hugo Chavez (Harnecker, 2005). By way of contrast, in the U.S., the health care crisis has, to date, produced a result analogous to that of the abolitionists. A huge difference with either the earlier abolition example, or the Venezuelan events, is that an organized progressive presence has neither been propelling changes in health care policy, nor substantially influencing the debate.

For a 21st Century Socialist effort to succeed in the U.S., like in Latin America, it must be constructed upon a grass-roots, bottom-up, rather than top-down, foundation. At the outset, this means generally greater emphasis placed on local rather than national elections. Given adequate base building, as discussed above, local elections offer substantially greater chance of influencing outcomes than do state or national races.

Once local foundations have been put in place, then it makes political sense to look seriously at state and national elections. A stronger local base raises the prospects of electing candidates who far more directly represent progressive values and social transformation, such as Kshama Sawant in Seattle. Then it also makes sense to look at possibilities that transcend the limitations of realignment.

Fortunately, many pieces of such a strategy are already available. A mass base must invariably involve labor, and there are signs the labor movement is coming to the realization that stable and rewarding lives for their members cannot be created through an illusory grand bargain with the self-serving interests of neoliberal capital. This requires adoption of a social, or social justice unionism, in place of a business unionism that cannot rise to the challenges increasingly attacking labor (Fletcher, 2014; Fletcher & Gaspasin, 2008).

A social union approach is imperative not only for wider labor support, it is a necessary component in elaborating and communicating communal needs in keeping with the prerogatives of 21st Century Socialism. There must be reciprocal relations between labor and the community. There are community-based developments that are reaching across the aisle to labor, or have tremendous power to do so.

These include recent actions and events identified as a "new populism," the Moral Mondays protests against unmet community needs now growing across the southeast, and the efforts of National People's Action to import such concerns into the political process (Dean, 2014; Dubose, 2014; Hickey, 2014; H. Targ, personal communication, March 24, 2014). There are abundant issues to organize around and alternative agendas upon which to draw, such as the Green New Deal (Green New Deal Group, 2014; Hickey, 2014).

What should be done with regard to these challenges? Socialists must assess what constitute important socioeconomic issues that will galvanize people in conjunction with specific and viable strategy and tactics that will mobilize them. Generalities will not suffice to create what's workable and what's needed to implement 21st Century Socialism in the U.S.

In order for a substantial segment of the U.S. population to accept change, they must be convinced that such change is realistic. We have strong examples in our history: the abolitionist, civil rights, feminist, anti-war, and other movements have shown us how it's done. Today's challenge is to wed that history to the eminently workable examples our 21st Century Socialist Century brothers and sisters in Latin America have been providing us. This is daunting, but as Nelson Mandela told us, "there is no easy walk to freedom."

While much work will be local, we must think in terms of national themes and campaigns. Not all localities will be able, or want to work on priorities that might be set at the national level, but there should be some sense of what might be generally workable throughout the country, along with an ability to provide various forms of support and assistance. Hardt and Negri tell us "Each struggle remains singular and tied to its local conditions but at the same time is immersed in the common web... The new global cycle of struggles organizes and mobilizes the multitude." (2004, p. 217).

References

Clark, V.F. & Grove, S. (2013, September 12). What can we learn from Salvador Allende? New Left Project. Retrieved from http://www.newleft-project.org/index.php/site/article_comments/allendes_legacy

Dean, A. B. (2014, March 3). Challenging Democrats from the left: Progressive grass-roots tactics can go a long way in the primaries. AlJazeera America. Retrieved from http://america.aljazeera.com/opinions/2014/3/grassroots-democratsprogressivesprimaries.html

Dieterich, H. (2007). The socialism of the 21st Century. European Institute for Progressive Cultural Policies (eipcp). Retrieved from http://eipcp.net/transversal/0805/dieterich/en

Dubose, L. (2014, January 6). The politics of faith and fusion: Moral Monday in North Carolina. The Washington Spectator. Retrieved from http://washingtonspectator.org/index.php/Politics/the-politics-of-faith-and-fusion-moral-monday-in-north-carolina.html#.Uy-O2yjFmMM

Fletcher, B. (2014, March 10). Concept paper: Theses toward the development of left labor strategy. Organizing Upgrade: Engaging left organizers in strategic dialog. Retrieved from http://organizingupgrade.com/index.php/modules-menu/labor/item/1017-concept-paper-theses-toward-the-development-of-left-labor-strategy

Fletcher, B. & Gapasin, F. (2008). Solidarity divided: The crisis in organized labor and a new path toward social justice. Berkeley: University of California.

Green New Deal Group (2014). Core principles. Author. Retrieved from http://www.greennewdealgroup.org/?page_id=88

Hardt, M. & Negri, A. (2004). Multitude: War and democracy in the age of empire. NY: Penguin.

Harnecker, M. (2005). Understanding the Venezuelan revolution: Hugo Chavez talks to Marta Harnecker, translated by Chesa Boudin. NY: Monthly Review.

Harnecker, M. (2007). Rebuilding the left. London: Zed.

Harnecker, M. (2010). Latin America & Twenty-first century socialism, Monthly Review (62)3. Retrieved from http://Monthlyreview.org/2010/07/01/latin-america-twenty-first-century-socialism

Hickey, R. (2014). The new populist movement. Huffington Post. Retrieved from http://www.huffingtonpost.com/roger-hickey/the-new-populist-movement_b_4899347.html

Lebowitz, M.A. (2014). Proposing a path to socialism: Two papers for Hugo Chavez. Monthly Review (65)10. Retrieved from http://monthlyreview.org/2014/03/01/proposing-path-socialism-two-papers-hugo-chavez

Mayer, H. (1998). All on fire: William Lloyd Garrison and the abolition of slavery. NY: St. Martin's.

Moulian, T. (2000). Socialismo del siglo XXI: La quinta via, Santiago, Chile: LOM.

Petras, J. (1969). Politics and social forces in Chilean development. Berkeley: University of California.

Petras, J. (2008, May 14). Salvador Allende and Hugo Chavez: Similarities and differences on the "national road to socialism." The James Petras website. Retrieved from http://petras.lahaine.org/?p=1734

Press TV. (2012, September 12). Venezuela's Chavez pays tribute to former Chilean President Salvador Allende. Retrieved from http://www.presstv.com/detail/2012/09/12/261223/chavez-former-chilean-president-allende/

Progressive Democrats of America (2013, June 28). Basic Principles. Progressive Democrats of America website. Retrieved from http://www.pdamerica.org/about-pda/basic-principles

Quinones, N. (2014, March 17). Court declares ruling party candidate El Salvador's president-elect. CNN. Retrieved from http://www.cnn.com/2014/03/17/world/americas/el-salvador-elections/

Jay D. Jurie is an associate professor of public administration and urban planning at the University of Central Florida. He has been a member of the chapter council and a statewide delegate to the United Faculty of Florida, AFT-NEA, and is a CCDS National Coordinating Committee member.

Solar Communism Revisited

By David Schwartzman

In this article on solar power and communism from 1996, I focus on the relevance of thermodynamics with its concept of entropy. In Solar Communism, I discuss the lack of a full conceptualization of the technological basis of an ecosocialist transition to a future global society. I argue that an historical materialist account of this transition and a vision of this future global society should encompass its full materiality, in both the technological and social senses of that term. Socialist or Marxist political economy is necessary but not sufficient in itself to advance a vision of 21st Century Socialism.

Twelve years later I again addressed the concept of entropy because even some Marxists did not get it right (Schwartzman, 2008). The natural, physical and informational sciences in particular, climatology, ecology, biogeochemistry, and thermodynamics must be fully engaged. These sciences will inform the technologies of renewable energy, green production, and agroecologies, whose infrastructure are to replace the present unsustainable mode. Since the publication of the article below in 1996, renewable energy technologies have advanced to a degree that they are being rapidly implemented around the world, but this growth is still coupled with the unsustainable rise of global fossil fuel consumption.

In the article, I recognized the growing threat of rising greenhouse gases derived from burning fossil fuels. In the nearly twenty years since this essay was published, this threat has grown into a global crisis of unprecedented magnitude.

Humanity and existing biodiversity are now facing a huge challenge in this the first half of the 21st century. Shall civilization emerge in a new mode, with the end of what Marx called our prehistory, the rule of capital on our planet, or shall we plunge into a deep abyss of climate hell, climate catastrophe, for the few who survive? This is the great bifurcation ahead, and the outcome is not possible to predict. Only transnational class struggle on a scale not witnessed in human history has any chance of avoiding the abyss (Schwartzman 2013a, b).

There are actually two major threats to human civilization. The first is that of nuclear war, which would be deadly even if localized, because of resulting climatic impact on agriculture. The second threat is catastrophic climate change (C3). C3 is very likely inevitable if carbon emissions to the atmosphere are not rapidly and radically reduced and if the already unsafe atmospheric level of carbon dioxide is not reduced by sequestration technologies to a safe level.

Paradoxically, however, we are also privileged to confront this challenge, since the process of removing these threats raises the possibility of ending the rule of capital on our planet.

But it is increasingly clear that only with a radical shift to a global regime of peace and cooperation will it be possible to implement an effective C3 prevention program. The threats of C3 and nuclear war pose an unprecedented opportunity to end the rule of capital, because the main obstacle to elimination of these threats is the MIC, the Military Industrial (Fossil Fuel, Nuclear, State Terror and Surveillance) Complex at the core of real existing capitalism (Schwartzman 2009). Thus, the challenge to dissolve the MIC puts an ecosocialist transition on the agenda for humanity—an ecosocialist transition out of prehistory and into a new global civilization, solar communism in the 21st Century.

The global North should transition to a simpler lifestyle, e.g. mass transit, bicycle transport in place of cars, smaller homes, and a great reduction in the consumption of obsolescent gadgets—the endless creation of manufactured desire driven by the reproduction of capital. If the transformation of agriculture to fossil fuel-free agroecologies that are situated closer to population centers is included, this degrowth translates into lower energy consumption in the global North, resulting in a higher quality of life with a more healthful environment, cleaner air, water, and organic food, free of the chemicals, and genetic contamination now inherent in industrial/GMO agriculture.

But the world needs more, not less energy consumption than now, with most of humanity, living in the global South receiving a significant increase, reaching the rough minimum of 3.5 kilowatt/person. Note that reaching this minimum is necessary but not sufficient for acquiring the highest life expectancy, as several petroleum-exporting countries in the Mid-East as well as Russia now fall well below that goal. Life expectancy for the United States is likewise below most industrial countries of the global North. Income inequality is robustly correlated with bad health and must be reduced to achieve the world standard life expectancy and

quality of life. Supplying the minimum 3.5 kilowatt/person for the present world population of 7 billion people requires a delivery equivalent to
25 trillion watts, with the present delivery equal to 18 trillion watts.

This is the critical challenge of a Global Green New Deal (Schwartzman,
2011). Creating a renewable energy infrastructure to supply this level
of energy consumption is not only possible, but also imperative in order
to eliminate the energy poverty now affecting the majority of humanity
living in the global South AND to confront the challenge of implementing a prevention program that has any chance of avoiding catastrophic
climate change. Given the global North's historic responsibility for the
threat of catastrophic climate change, transfer of wind/solar capacity to
the global South from the global North is imperative. With 1 to 2% of
current annual consumption of energy (85% derived from fossil fuels) being used for wind/solar power creation per year, a global-scale transition
can be achieved in no more than 30 years, with the complete elimination
of anthropogenic carbon emissions derived from energy consumption
to the atmosphere and the provision of the minimum per capita energy
consumption level required for state-of-the-science life expectancy level
for all (Schwartzman and Schwartzman, 2011, 2013).

Solar Communism

Science & Society, Vol. 60, No. 3, Fall 1996, 307-331

The main purpose of this paper is to provoke a rethinking of the Marxian
concept of communism as a prospect for global civilization, particularly
with respect to its energetic basis and the problem of optimizing society-nature relations now and in the future. This reinterrogation requires
an understanding of the physical concepts of energy and entropy (i.e.,
thermodynamics). I will argue that these considerations lead to the conclusion that both solarization of the global economy and the application
of the containment and precautionary principles are necessary for the
ultimate realization of planetary communism, and these requirements
should inform a viable socialist strategy.

Ever since Georgescu-Roegen (1971) revived entropy as a preeminent indicator of the ultimate limits of a growing economy, entropy has been employed
to impute a theoretical physical basis for social prognostication (see Martinez-Alier, 1987). A considerable literature has appeared (see Daly and Cobb,
1989, for a representative use of Georgescu Roegen's concepts; Rifkin, 1980,
1989, for a popularization). Georgescu-Roegen's writings have had wide influence on leading contemporary environmental theorists, such as Herman
Daly, a seminal thinker on "ecological economics", as well as those with a
Marxist perspective (e.g., Altvater, 1993, 1994; Dryzek, 1994).

However, a fog of confusion has been generated by Georgescu-Roegen's conceptual foundation. I will attempt to dissipate this fog, leaving visible what is of theoretical and practical usefulness to the issue at hand, the rethinking of the material basis for Marxian communism and prerequisites to its achievement.

We will begin with a look back at the formulation of the concept of entropy and the theory of the heat death of the universe, and its reincarnation in the use/misuse of thermodynamic entropy in contemporary studies of the environmental limits of economic activity.

1. Entropy and heat death

The thermodynamic concept of entropy arose directly from Carnot's theorization of the operation of the steam engine (see Cardwell, 1989). This theorization led to the formulation of the Second Law Of Thermodynamics: the entropy of an isolated system (i.e., closed to transfer of energy or matter) must increase as a result of any change therein. There are dozens of equivalent ways of expressing the second law (the first states the conservation of energy). One other formulation is relevant here: heat cannot flow from a cooler to a hotter reservoir without any other change (i.e., work must be done). The increase of entropy is equivalent to the increased inability of an isolated system to do work, resulting from the degradation of low entropy energy into waste heat (an isolated system is defined as being closed to both energy and matter transfers in or out, while a closed system is only closed to matter transfers). Entropy has been loosely defined as the measure of the disorder of a system. More precisely, thermodynamic entropy is the "randomized state of energy that is unavailable to do work" (Lehninger, 1965). In the classical interpretation, ultimately, all processes in the universe must lead to its "heat death" as the potential for further change is ended. As Cardwell put it:

"The cosmic role of heat, first discerned at the end of the eighteenth century and eloquently described by writers like Fourier and Carnot had thus, by way of Joule, Rankine and Kelvin, achieved its final definition by Clausius. This is not a balanced, symmetrical, self-perpetuating universe, as the development of rational mechanics, building on the foundations of Newton's System of the World, seemed so confidently to indicate. It is a universe tending inexorably to doom, to the atrophy of a 'heat death', in which no energy at all will be available although none will have been destroyed; and the complementary condition is that the entropy of the universe will be at its maximum." (Cardwell, 1989, 273.)

Not surprisingly, heat death was not accepted by Engels and most later Marxists, since this scenario embodies a deeply pessimistic perspective of natural evolution. Engels' (1987) decisive rejection is found in

Dialectics of Nature. He asserts that the heat radiated into space must by some as yet unknown mechanism be re-utilized in the eternal cycle since motion in the universe is inexhaustible (see 561-563, 334). Haeckel (1900) shared Engels' view of the inexhaustibility of motion in the universe while accepting the applicability of the Second Law in local systems (246-247). The categorical rejection of heat death became accepted canon in official Marxism-Leninism:

> "the "theory of the heat death of the universe" is completely unfounded and ignores the law of conservation (sic) and transformation of energy which asserts the indestructibility of motion not only quantitatively but also qualitatively, i.e., that motion cannot exist in only one form." (Afanasyev, n.d., 69)

And similarly:

> "For systems consisting of an infinitely great number of particles (the Universe or the world as a whole) the concept of the most probable state loses its meaning (in infinitely large systems all states are equally probable). By taking into account the role of gravitation, cosmology arrives at the conclusion that the Entropy of the Universe grows without tending to any maximum (the state of thermal balance). Modern science proves the complete groundlessness of the conclusions of the allegedly inevitable thermal balance and "thermal death" of the world." (Frolov, 1984, 126-127.) (Note that another assumption of official Marxism-Leninism, the infinity of the universe, is used here to prove the invalidity of heat death.)

Turmoil over Theory

Soviet physicists and philosophers rejected heat death from a variety of positions. Even the great Lev Landau, not noted for his obsequious adherence to Marxism-Leninism, apparently rejected heat death from considerations of relativistic thermodynamics (Graham, 1987, 500, n. 39). Similarly, the eminent physicist and Einstein scholar B. Kuznetsov could not swallow heat death:

> "Philosophy, in particular the philosophy of Engels, and 19th century statistical physics advanced rather convincing arguments against thermal death. Modern science, the theory of relativity and relativistic cosmology and, to no lesser extent, quantum mechanics, forces us to interpret the thermodynamics of the Universe from new standpoints that assumedly eliminate the inevitability of thermal death, although they still do not offer any concrete and unequivocal conception of the cosmic mechanism of forming temperature gradients, contrasted to thermal death" (Kuznetsov, 1977, 34.)

In other words, we are still waiting for the mechanism Engels was convinced could turn waste heat to low entropy energy! While a near consensus of rejection was held by the materialist camp, particularly of Marxist persuasion, supporters of the heat death scenario in the 19th and 20th century put it to good use in a broad range of ideological interventions. This history is discussed extensively by Martinez-Alier (1987) and will not be pursued in any detail here. One example will suffice: the argument for vitalism based on the purported anti-entropic quality of life and its evolution (e.g., Henry Adams, following Haeckel; see Martinez-Alier). The confusion embodied in this position is easily clarified by the fact that a living organism is an open system - the entropy in the environment therefore increases as a debt for any internal process - but this erroneous position lives on in many contemporary treatments (e.g., writings by creationists, followers of Lyndon LaRouche and by those who should know better).

Contemporary cosmologists have taken a fresh look at the heat death scenario. There is continued debate as to its validity in the context of cosmological theories of inflation, collapsing and expanding universes (see Davies, 1977, Barrow and Tipler, 1988, Coveney and Highfield, 1990, Barrow, 1994). For example, in a universe that will expand forever (cosmologists are still not sure whether our universe is in this class) the actual growth of entropy may never equal the maximum potential entropy, thus heat death may be indefinitely postponed (Barrow, 1994). With the increasing strangeness of new theories in theoretical physics it would be no surprise that the old heat death scenario may be reinterpreted in the future in a radically different form.

Whatever the eventual reinterpretation of ultimate heat death, its invocation in the present context and inconceivably far into the future is irrelevant to an understanding of the ubiquitous emergence of ordered (so-called "anti-entropic") systems in the universe (e.g., stars) and here on earth (e.g., life and society). This spontaneous self-organization of matter is consistent with the second law, since entropy always increases in the self-organizing system plus its environment. Ordering and its maintenance within the system generates a entropic flux passing into the local environment (see Bertalanffy, 1968, 4041; on the thermodynamics of self-organization see Prigogine and Stengers, 1984).

The Earth is of course not an isolated system in a thermodynamic sense because of the incoming solar flux to the surface (and an equivalent radiant energy flux back out to space), but is closed to matter transfers (except for the trivial meteorite and space vehicle fluxes). (Footnote: We neglect here the energy flux coming from below the Earth's surface, arising from radioactive decay in the crust and mantle. While much smaller than the solar flux, this energy source is the basis of internally generated geologic activity such as volcanism, and is critical to the long term evolution of the crust and biosphere.)

Therefore, like the natural biosphere powered by solar energy, the ordering and maintenance of the material creation of human activity on the Earth's surface can continue far into the future by the export of an entropic flux into space, provided a long term energy source (the sun) is utilized.

2. Ecocatastrophe: the reincarnation of entropy in social prognostication

First the heat death of the universe, now immanent ecocatastrophe. In his writings, Georgescu-Roegen (see 1971) bridged the gap between entropy's earlier use and the contemporary interpretation bearing on economics, energy and the environment. (Footnote: Ironically, Georgescu-Roegen actually leaned at one point (1971; he changes his mind in 1976, 8) to rejecting the heat death scenario because of his favoring the steady-state cosmology (both entropy and matter are created and destroyed) while invoking entropic limits to economic activity, in his critique of neo-classical economic theory ("the ultimate fate of the universe is not the Heat Death... but a much grimmer state - Chaos"). Thus, while wavering on accepting the classical Marxist concept of the inexhaustibility of matter in motion on the scale of the universe, Georgescu-Roegen rejects its neo-classical analogue (economic cycle in a finite world without a limit) on the scale of the economy)

According to Georgescu-Roegen neo-classical theory conflicts with the second law: "the economic process materially consists of a transformation of low entropy into high entropy, i.e., into waste" (1971, 18) and as low entropy resources run out, especially fossil fuels, economic activity becomes increasingly limited by the accumulation of waste (pollution) and scarcity of energy (for a defense of the "orthodox" position see Arrow, 1981). Following Georgescu-Roegen's ideas, Daly and Cobb (1989) contend that we are rapidly approaching the physical limits to the further growth of the world economy since the growth of physical throughput will inevitably deplete the energy, materials and space on which it depends, with the concomitant progressive destruction of the biosphere. Future knowledge cannot "remove limits on the physical scale of the economy resulting from finitude, entropy, and ecological dependence" (Daly and Cobb, 1989, 199). (Footnote: This analysis has been recently critiqued (Boucher et al., 1993, drawing on Commoner's, 1990, arguments; also see Sagoff, 1995 and Daly, 1995 for a recent debate), and Daly himself has shown some indications that he has backed off from his original formulation, though it is repeated in the revised edition of Daly and Cobb.)

Furthermore, Georgescu-Roegen claims to have discovered a Fourth Law of Thermodynamics:

"A. Unavailable matter cannot be recycled.
B. A closed system (i.e, a system that cannot exchange matter with the environment) cannot perform work indefinitely at a constant rate." (Georgescu-Roegen, 1989, 304).

This purported law, however, is sheer nonsense since it neglects to account for the possible flow of energy through the system which is defined as closed but not isolated.

By converting low entropy, high temperature energy (e.g., solar radiation) to high entropy, low temperature heat, work can be produced to recycle indefinitely (see e.g., Bianciardi et al., 1993). Unfortunately, many recent discussions repeat this erroneous concept (e.g., Altvater, 1994, Dryzek, 1994). Interestingly, in one paper Georgescu-Roegen (1976) defines "closed" as entailing "no exchange of matter or energy with [the] environment" (recall that in thermodynamics this is defined as an "isolated" system, not "closed"); he still maintains that according to the second law matter along with energy is subject to "irrevocable dissipation" (8).

This confusion may be linked to his pessimistic view on harnessing solar energy (see below), since the latter is the relevant energy flux to consider for the closed but not isolated system containing economic activity on the earth's surface. This distinction between closed and isolated systems is also central to the problem of optimizing society's relation to nature (an issue to be discussed latter in the paper).

In Rifkin's hands (1980, 1989) the entropy concept is extended to its apocryphal limits: entropy as a pollutant, as an indicator of cosmic disorder, the inexorable outcome of all economic activity, the mother of ecocatastrophe (note that Georgescu-Roegen enthusiastically endorses Rifkin's treatment of the subject, in his After word to Rifkin's book). To his credit, he does outline the necessity of shifting to a solar economy, albeit with a strong Luddite flavor. Rifkin favors a pre-industrial global population of less than 1 billion people (1989 edition, 254), and rejects the use of computers since they generate entropy (1989 edition, 190-191)!

While Georgescu-Roegen's views on entropy and the economy are questionable, his work has stimulated welcome and wide-ranging debate on physical-environmental constraints of economic activity. As we will see in the next section, his critique is particularly fertile for an economy based on non-renewable energy.

3. Thermodynamic entropy: its use/misuse and redundancy in ecological economics

Before going further, it is helpful to distinguish between the entropy of thermodynamics, statistical mechanics and information theory/computation (see Proops, 1987; Rothman, 1989). The latter two "entropies", particularly the statistical mechanical, have deep, though debatable connections to thermodynamic entropy. The entropy of information theory, especially as a measure of concentration to a set of probabilities (see Proops, 1987), has found wide and useful application in economics and the social sciences. In this discussion we will only consider the application of classical thermodynamic entropy to economics and the environment.

Thus, I will not consider the interesting attempts to apply non-equilibrium and far-from-equilibrium thermodynamics to understand self-organization in the economic and social realms (see e.g., Dyke, 1988 and M. O'Connor, 1991).

A fundamental criticism of Georgescu-Roegen's (and Rifkin's) invocation of entropy is that material/energy transformations in an economy take place far from equilibrium, thus it is incorrect to use the thermodynamic entropy of near equilibrium processes for its description (see Morowitz, 1986). An analogous criticism has been made of its similar use in modeling biotic and climatic processes, but deep insights can be obtained from the near-equilibrium approximation if its limits are appreciated (see Schwartzman et al., 1994).

Is Waste Heat Reusable?

Does the thermodynamic entropy concept really give us any insight into the environmental effect of economic activity? As a first order deduction: in an economy run on fossil fuel energy, which of course has finite reserves, the second law simply indicates that energy to do work is not renewable, i.e., you cannot "reuse" waste heat ad infinitum (true of waste heat from using solar energy as well) nor can you regenerate the low entropy energy reserve (with solar energy the sun does this for you!) (see Rothman's critique of Rifkin; Rothman, 1989).

Beyond this basic insight, the concept is really redundant to a simple consideration of the energy budget alone in understanding anthropogenic heat pollution and the enhanced greenhouse, but is useful in considering gaining insight into issues of recycling and pollution and energy conservation. (Footnote: Evaluation of alternative ways of accomplishing the same goal (e.g., heating a house) using second law efficiencies (the

ratio of the least available work that could have done the job to the actual available work used to do the job) can lead to substantial savings of
energy; see Commoner, 1976, and Ford et al., 1975).)

Consider the energy budget at the Earth's surface. Globally the solar
energy flux to the atmosphere/surface equals the flux radiating back to
space, similarly for energy budget at the surface itself. Most of this solar
radiation (visible light) is irreversibly converted to heat radiation (infra-
red) at the surface (other natural sources of heat such as geothermal are
trivial compared to the solar flux). If the Earth surface were perfectly
reflecting, with an albedo equal to one, then no heat radiation would be
emitted. The natural greenhouse effect is caused by the absorption of
heat radiation by molecules of water and carbon dioxide in the atmosphere and its re-radiation to the surface.

Were it not for this greenhouse effect the Earth's surface would be about
$30^\circ C$ cooler. Any economy based on energy sources other than the direct solar flux impinging on the Earth's surface (i.e., fossil fuels, the
stored solar energy of past geological epochs, as well as nuclear and
geothermal energy) must inevitably alter the heat budget by the emis-
sion of heat radiation over and above the natural flux from the surface.
Such direct anthropogenic heat pollution presently accounts for 0.03%
of the solar flux impinging on the land surface (Smil, 1992); localized
however in cities and industrial centers, it produces the heat island effect, the elevation of temperature in and around cities (see further discussion of the latter in the next footnote).

Much more serious is the well-known, enhanced greenhouse effect resulting from anthropogenic carbon dioxide and other gaseous emissions
such as methane (see Lovejoy, this issue). A solar-based world economy
would not affect the Earth's surface heat budget (except in its initial
"parasitic" phase, relying on fossil fuels and nuclear power), providing
the tapping of solar energy involves no net transfers of carbon dioxide,
methane or other greenhouse gases to the atmosphere/ocean system
(e.g. by deforestation, flooding from big hydropower projects). Tapping
solar energy directly merely utilizes a small part of the immense flux
to do work which ultimately would be simply converted into waste heat
anyway, as in the case of natural heat budget (anthropogenic albedo
changes such as making the surface darker may result in changes in
the surface heat budget, but globally they are small compared to other
effects).

Regarding the energy cost of recycling, cleaning up and/or restoring the
biosphere, and mining/refining mineral ores with increasingly scarce
concentrated sources, the same argument applies, since fossil fuels,
nuclear and geothermal all insult the biosphere by incremental heat as

well as by pollution effects (e.g., nuclear power results in significant thermal pollution of bodies of water along with the other well-known effects, nuclear power has been largely parasitic on fossil fuels). A non-solar economy must generate additional insults in the cleanup or recycling process, since its very use must pollute thermally and materially. (Footnote: These effects are of course on top of the problem of diminishing reserves of fossil fuels (see Lovejoy, this issue), finite lifetimes of geothermal reservoirs, all which make the "soft path" essential into the next century. A practical source of fusion energy might eventually be powered by the essentially inexhaustible supply of deuterium in the oceans, with minimal impact on the environment other than incremental heat production.

Even if some form of "cold fusion" should ultimately be developed the incremental heat problem will remain. For an anthropogenic heat production of some 100 times the present, a 2oC increase in the global mean surface temperature is estimated (Kellogg, 1978). However, since the release of anthropogenic heat would likely be highly localized, the heat island effect would be significantly magnified at production levels far below that value.) This is not a necessary outcome for a solar-based economy. It is curious that no recent literature on this subject makes this simple observation in a clearly stated argument that emphasizes its profound significance. Georgescu-Roegen (1976) makes the essential point at least once, but fails to develop it (in later writings, such as his after word in Rifkin (1980, 1989), he is less optimistic about the prospects for direct use of solar energy, seeing it as "parasites of the current technology" (1989, 304):

"any use of solar energy is pollution-free. For whether this energy is used or not, its ultimate fate is the same, namely, to become dissipated heat that maintains the thermodynamic equilibrium between the globe and outer space at a propitious temperature." In a footnote to this passage he points out: "One necessary qualification: even the use of solar energy may disturb the climate if the energy is released in another place than where collected. The same is true for a difference in time, but this case is unlikely to have any practical importance." (Georgescu-Roegen, 1976, 28).

In a more recent publication (Daly, 1992) defending Georgescu-Roegen, Daly makes no reference to this concept, although he comes close in two places (Daly, 1991, 226, cited in Haavelmo and Hansen, 1992, 42). More typical is Jacobs' (1991) treatment. He argues that "solving the entropic problem" lies in the direct collection of solar energy, because it generates little or no pollution in use (115), but indicates in a footnote "All use of energy generates thermal pollution (heat)" This begs the question since what counts is incremental heat over and above the natural flux off the Earth's surface.

However, there is an entropy concept which sheds some light on the impact of recycling and pollution, as well as the energy requirements of mining and refining mineral ores, one that is alluded to above, the entropy of mixing. Entropy is produced in any actually occurring process, including mixing heterogeneous substances. Faber et al., 1987, employ the concept of entropy of mixing in their treatment of resource extraction and pollution. A simple example is instructive: much more energy is required to recover the perfume molecules from a room than to transfer the perfume in a closed container. The entropy of mixing is a measure of the energy cost to recycle or restore the biosphere (e.g., partially restore strip mined land); the greater the dispersal of recyclable material or scale of physical disruption, the greater is the energy cost.

It is also an index of the energy required for extraction of an element from an ore; in general, the lower the grade of ore (concentration), the greater the energy required. With pollutants, the relation of the entropy of mixing to adverse environmental impact is more complex. The same relation for recyclable material of course applies to the energy cost of cleaning up pollution. However, the more dilution occurs for a given amount of pollutant (e.g. Pb), the higher the entropy of mixing (for unmixed Pb sitting in a container, the entropy of mixing is zero), but the lower the impact on the biosphere, below a certain threshold concentration. Above this concentration, however, the impact is spatially widened and may become global (e.g., could chlorinated hydrocarbons, globally dispersed, be responsible for the apparent disruption of hormonal balance in various animals, including humans?).

Qualitative factors are of course critical to the actual impact of a pollutant. These factors include toxicity, biodegradability, residence time, instability, is the pollutant naturally occurring or artificial?, etc. There are analogous considerations for the energy required for extraction/refining a mineral resource (e.g., chemical and physical state, the technology employed). These qualitative factors have no simple parameterization in an expression for entropy of mixing (see Faber et al., 1987, 124). Even in a solar economy, some pollution could occur (of course adverse effects on workers and the community already occur in the embryonic renewable energy industry; witness Silicon Valley). The concepts discussed will have utility then, and during the solarization transition.

4. Solar communism?

Human needs, nature's needs. The relevance of the preceding discussion to a rethinking of the Marxist concept of communism will now be examined. According to the classical tradition, the communist socioeconomic formation can only be reached with an end to scarcity, presupposing an abundant and continuous source of energy. Is this concept now imaginable in any plausible sense that could motivate an effective political practice? In what follows, and despite anticipated derision from the postmodernist camp, I will argue for such a vision, one of a future that also necessarily entails the utilization of the full potential of the information revolution and a radical modification of present society-nature relations.

We begin with a consideration of human needs, since the promise of their satisfaction is central to Marx's concept of communism ("from each according to his ability, to each according to his needs"). Utopian thinkers historically have always postulated that human needs could be met at existing technological levels, but for class exploitation and oppression. The technology of every age has its utopia (e.g., Kropotkin, 1989, at the beginning of this century). Of course, each age, particularly contemporary capitalism has expanded the realm of perceived human need. Human needs are of course problematic, generated by political struggle and cultural history. Beyond physiological necessities (as the number of calories, vitamins etc. needed for optimal health, itself not entirely without uncertainty) and the other conditions for healthful life such as an unpolluted environment, adequate shelter, and loving relationships, our needs, both material and spiritual, are largely social constructs.

Of course even the prospect of substantially extending the human life span will be a social construct, while becoming an arguably new entitlement for all human beings. Doyal and Gough (1991) have eloquently argued for an objective basis underlying common human needs worldwide. Nevertheless, many "needs" under capitalism are obvious creations of consumerism, itself a direct outcome of the unfettered reproduction of capital, and must be the terrain of political struggle since these "needs" in turn reproduce unhealthful conditions for both humans and the biosphere (e.g., polluting cars, wasteful packaging, high fat diets etc.). Further, both the ability and needs of a healthy biosphere are not without some uncertainty: for example, what constitutes sustainable yields of wood, fish, how much of the biosphere should be left relatively pristine in "biosphere reserves"?; etc.

An end to scarcity, at least in respect to objectively defined needs, could arguably only occur in a planetary civilization, given the great disparity in the human condition at present. Here again we can anticipate the continual creation of new human needs, with the elimination of old ones (e.g., with the extension of human life span, new possibilities for travel, like vacations on Mars!). However, all this speculation surely appears as escapist fantasy in face of the colossal challenges facing humankind today, with millions barely surviving even in the cities of the industrial world.

With the new level of anthropogenic impacts of capitalism on the bio-sphere, the "second contradiction" of capitalism as theorized by James O'Connor (1988; see also numerous articles since then in same journal), between the forces/relations and conditions of production (above all nature, but also the artificial environment, which of course includes the workplace and urban communities), has now emerged with global con-sequence. The second contradiction of capitalism forces a reexamina-tion of the very principle proposed to guide a communist society: "From each according to her ability, to each according to her needs". Should not "each" and "her" now refer to both human beings and nature (eco-systems)? Further, if "socialism" as a transition to communism is to be viable, this new principle must arguably be progressively applied to this mixed social formation, between two modes of production. Indeed, the convergence of the green and socialist movements may be for the same reason a necessary condition for the very possibility of opening a path to communism via socialism.

Energetics. But what are the implications of the ecological question with-in socialist theory to the energetic basis of human civilization meeting both human and nature's needs? Bernal (1959) speaking from another age (only three decades ago!) believed that a source of abundant cheap energy (nuclear energy) could soon "liberate man completely from want" (270). It would be "freely available as air and light are today" (49), ironi-cally echoing President Eisenhower's promise to the U.N. some years before. He observed that one possible drawback in its greatly expanded use was overheating the Earth's surface. Presciently, Bernal noted the following concerning solar energy:

"For this source of energy is so diffused that the real difficulty is in find-ing any cheap way of concentrating it from large surfaces...This may not always be so difficult. Indeed, by the use of cheap thermo-electric sub-stances transforming the heat of sunlight directly into electricity, it may very soon be possible - at least in sunny climates to rival atomic energy in cheapness and certainly in simplicity and safety." (46.)

After Chernobyl and escalating costs of electricity from nuclear energy, the nuclear option appears much less attractive as an energetic basis of global civilization. What then of solar?

I contend "planetary solar communism", harnessing the power of pres-ent and soon-to-be- developed technologies of information and renew-able energy, is a plausible vision of future global civilization.

A transition to renewable energy from fossil fuels and nuclear energy, the "soft path" advocated by A. Lovins, will make possible a radically new global economy, sustainable and growing. As Barry Commoner (1990) has pointed out, we are far from approaching physical limits to growth. The world economy could increase its energy consumption say 10-fold by simply tapping 1% of the solar radiation now impinging on the earth's land surface without altering the present heat budget of the earth's surface via greenhouse gas emissions or direct waste heat production (unlike the use of fossil fuels and nuclear energy). The annual flux of solar radiation to the earth is approximately 10 times the total energy stored in the global coal resource or one million billion (1015) barrels of crude oil (Smil, 1991). Contrary to Daly and Cobb's (1989) generalization regarding the limits to economic activity, the use of solar energy will make possible an increase in the physical throughput (material processing) in the human-made technosphere without adverse impact on the biosphere, provided the production- consumption cycle is closed (i.e., recycling, waste-free technology). Actually, the restoration of the biosphere, along with the task of raising the quality of life of all to the highest world standards, may require a substantial increase in global energy consumption, until this transition is completed.

Confronting Scepticism

Nevertheless, there is deep skepticism with respect to the possibility of solarizing a modern industrial economy. Georgescu-Roegen viewed the technology of the direct collection of solar radiation as "feasible" but not "viable", i.e., possible to construct and operate, but only by continuing to rely on fossil fuel energy inputs:

"all solar recipes known at present are parasites of the current technologies and therefore, will cease to be applicable when their host is no longer alive" (1981, 70-71). He argues that "in spite of the unusually large funds spent by public and private agencies bent on finding a solution to the unavoidable exhaustion of fossil fuels, it has not been possible to set up even a pilot plant in which solar collectors of one kind or another would be produced only with the energy collected by that conversion." (198).

These views are surprising, given the fact that the utilization of fossil fuels was once "parasitic" on recently collected photosynthetic energy (i.e., food for humans, beasts of burden and wood). Nevertheless, Georgescu-Roegen's views on solar technology's viability are apparently shared by several later writers influenced by his thinking:

"Solar energy in no way offers a "Promethian" discovery like the harnessing of fire in the Neolithic revolution or the concentration of steam for energy in the Industrial Revolution. For solar energy converters require so much space and so many inputs that the gain in useful energy would be outweighed by the investment in energy and materials." (Altvater, 1993, 223-224).

However, Daly is not convinced Georgescu-Roegen is right on this issue (see Daly and Umana, 1981, 174). Even Arrow, Georgescu-Roegen's "orthodox" economist opponent is more optimistic:

"We may evaluate new sources of energy in ways which use current prices based on current uses of nonrenewable sources of energy. Thus, photovoltaic solar cells are
produced with conventional energy sources and priced accordingly. These availabilities and prices could not persist into an era in which all energy is solar. The means of acquiring solar energy would themselves have to be produced with the aid of solar energy...It seems very likely to me that even with existing techniques a world run purely on renewable energy (a stationary state) would be feasible. No doubt it would be a considerably poorer world than we have now, but we might expect technological improvements to remedy that. After all, no great breakthroughs in scientific or technological principles are needed, much less than for successful power from fusion; all that is required is a series of improvements which have quite frequently accompanied great expansions of an industry." (113.)

On the issue of "viability" of direct collection technology, one recent study (Kuwano, 1994) estimates an energy payback time (number of years that are required for solar cell modules to generate the same amount of electric energy as consumed in their fabrication) of 1-4 years for two different silicon-based photovoltaic systems. Photovoltaics now have a bright future as a preeminent renewable energy source (see Stone, 1993). Land use requirements are large, but not inconceivable, particularly if revolutionary new advances in photovoltaic conversion efficiency come to fruition (The Scientist, 1994). Stone estimates that all electricity generation requirements in the U.S. could be met by present silicon-based photovoltaic modules on a land area 140 x 140km, an area far less than that presently used for U.S. military installations (Golob and Brus, 1993). (Footnote: Plausible scenarios for the soft path are found in Pimentel et al., 1994 (for the United States) and Boyle, 1994 (for the world). For a critique of other technical objections see Schwartzman, 1995, and Sagoff, 1995, for a rebuttal of pessimistic views on solarization. Further discussion of the plausibility of a solarization scenario is found in Lovejoy (this issue).)

A future global economy energized by the direct collection of solar radiation, at high conversion efficiencies would be, to use that old Hegelian-Marxist metaphor, a negation of the negation of pre-industrial energetics powered by recent/current solar flux via photosynthesis, highly inefficient, the latter being first negated by industrial society powered by fossil fuels which released stored solar energy trapped millions of years ago (see Smil, 1991, for conversion efficiencies and multifold details).

Environmental Policy

Solarization of the global economy is a necessary but not sufficient step towards radically limiting the environmental and ecological impacts of economic activity. I propose reconsideration of a radical solution to optimizing the relation of the technosphere to ecosphere: maximizing the containment of the technosphere, as originally argued by Taylor and Humpstone (1973), in a seminal, if now forgotten book. The technosphere is defined as the human created and modified environment while the ecosphere is the "natural" world (Commoner, 1990). (Footnote: The technosphere includes urban/suburban areas, roads, agricultural land, and forested land substantially modified by harvesting. Second growth forest (such as in much of New England, U.S.) is at the problematic boundary between the technosphere and ecosphere, since anthropogenic and natural perturbations often produce convergent results, but not necessarily at the same scale or speed (e.g., forest fires). However, to relativize humans and their technosphere as simply part of "nature" is an argument that can be used to justify any alteration of ecosystems as "natural" and therefore acceptable. The ecosphere and its subsystems ("ecosystems") exist with varying degrees of anthropogenic impact, that are increasingly well documented historically and spatially and distinguishable from natural processes (e.g., global pollution by lead, identified by isotopic tracing).) Other views of natural ecosystems absolutize aspects of their natural character; e.g., the phenomenon of temporary steady states is presumed to imply a state of permanent balance were it not for anthropogenic influences (Gore, 1992), an obsolete ecological concept (see Botkin, 1990).)

Today, the boundary between the technosphere and ecosphere is neither closed nor isolated (since they both exist on the Earth's surface, except in the most trivial sense they are presently closed with respect to the space environment, but not of course isolated because of the flux of radiation in and out). Implementation of solarization and the containment principle with respect to the technosphere will close the ecosphere to radiative inputs incremental to the surface fluxes, to inputs of substances and genetic information not naturally present (e.g., CFCs, chlorinated hydrocarbons, genetically engineered organisms) as well as to fluxes of naturally present substances above trivial levels compared to those in the ecosphere (e.g., nitrates; the anthropogenic flux of fixed nitrogen from fertilizer, power plants etc. is now approximately equal to the natural flux from nitrogen-fixing microbes and lightning).

The containment strategy is a marked departure from much of the Marxist (and Leninist) tradition. Marx (and Engels) wrote that "communism differs from all previous movements in that it overturns the basis of all earlier relations of production and intercourse, and for the first time consciously treats all natural premises as the creatures of men, strips them of their natural character and subjugates them to the power of individuals united." (Marx and Engels, 1947, 70).

"Really free working...is the most intense exertion. The work of material production can achieve this character only ... when it is of a scientific and at the same time general character, not merely human exertion as a specifically harnessed natural force, but exertion as a subject, which appears in the production process not in a merely natural, spontaneous form, but as an activity regulating all the forces of nature." (Marx, 1973, 611-612).

Frolov's (1989) position is typical for Leninists:

"It is the purposeful transformation of nature and optimization of biosphere on the basis of continued scientific and technological progress that will bring about harmonization of human interaction with nature" (Frolov, 1989, 12, italics in the original)

This view follows naturally from Vernadsky's concept of the noosphere, as a new stage of the global biosphere:

"Mankind taken as a whole is becoming a mighty geological force. There arises the problem of the reconstruction of the biosphere in the interests of freely thinking humanity as a single totality. This new state of the biosphere, which we approach without noticing it, is the noosphere." (Vernadsky, 1945, 9, italics in the original)

Vernadsky's conception of the noosphere converged with the ambitions of the socialist planners of the Soviet economy (Bailes, 1990), who were responsible for colossal industrial projects that resulted in enormous environmental destruction (Feshbach and Friendly, 1992; cf. Adabashev, 1966). Whether or not this outcome was "over determined" is another issue. Some of the biggest planned projects (e.g., the diversion of Siberian rivers to arid Soviet Central Asia) were narrowly averted as a result of the intervention of the Soviet ecological movement (Feshbach and Friendly, 1992).

Nevertheless, there is another legacy of Vernadsky, the science of biogeochemistry, which is of vital importance to understanding environmental impacts (e.g., global warming which is the product of anthropogenic effects on the biogeochemical cycle of carbon which consists of all the fluxes of carbon through surface systems, including the biomass) and optimizing the relation of society to nature (see Kamshilov, 1976). The incompleteness of our knowledge in this science, and especially the possibility of inherent unpredictability of anthropogenic impacts (Ayres,

1993) underlies the necessity for the containment and precautionary principles.

With the management of the global economy guided by these principles regulation and mastery of nature assumes a new content. No longer will nature be transformed and degraded. The ecosphere will be exploited as never before, but as a source of knowledge, and not material. Its biodiversity will be mined but not reduced. Knowledge of the ecosphere - its ecology, biogeochemical dynamics, biodiversity - will flow into the technosphere, driving its productive forces and internal transformation. For example, agricultural systems, a key component of the technosphere, will be transformed in multifold ways, with open field crops becoming polycultures, utilizing ecologic pest control ("agro ecology"; see Levins and Lewontin, 1985) and a big expansion of greenhouses, with potentially high productivity gains (see Taylor and Humpstone, 1973).

Containment of the technosphere is a radical application of the precautionary principle, as well as a solution to the problem of future generational representation in today's decisions, since it maximizes the preservation of the present ecosphere for the future. It is likewise a recognition of the inherent economic incommensurability of biospheric values, a recognition that appears impossible under unfettered capital reproduction, without real social governance of production and consumption (see discussion in Martinez-Alier, 1987, and Burkett, this issue). Containment does not necessarily mean a non-intervention policy to natural threats to the ecosphere, such as catastrophic volcanic eruptions, or impending large meteorite collisions (at least the latter could conceivably be averted by human intervention using nuclear weapons to divert the incoming body!).

Further, the reversal of global anthropogenic alterations (e.g., elevated levels of carbon dioxide in atmosphere) may require breaching the containment barrier (e.g., sequestering carbon dioxide using solar based technology), but such breaches should be made with great care and only under extraordinary conditions. Since no single containment wall is impermeable, and the technosphere is by definition for human habitation, the technosphere should employ non-toxic, closed cycle technologies. The physical limits to decentralization of human settlement will likely be imposed by the globally agreed upon allotment of relatively pristine biosphere; one plausible scenario is the construction of Soleri's arcologies (1969), compact "cities in the sky" coexisting with dispersed small relatively self- sufficient communities/bioregions embedded in restored biosphere. Only the most naive can believe that something like the scenario outlined above could be achieved without a powerful transnational political movement organized at the grassroots. (Footnote: The relevance of the population growth question to technosphereecosphere relations deserves an extended treatment, which will not be attempted here. Implicit in this paper is the assumption that rates of population growth and the limits to the presumed carrying capacity of the biosphere are largely dependent functions of political economy and technosphere/ecosphere relations, and not independent factors driving the "environmental crisis". Even quite poor states in the Third World have achieved remarkable reductions in population growth under governments which foster high literacy, empowerment of women and provision of basic needs (see Sen, 1994). See Lovejoy, this issue, for further discussion.)

Information technology. A vision of solar communism also requires the realization of the full potential of the information revolution, opening up the possibility for the flowering of human creative life activity for all. Bernal (1959), like others of his time, predicted the vast expansion of automation in industry and service sectors, guided by the electronic computer, which would have the potential to substantially shorten the work week. We are now deep in this technological revolution. Of course, it would be naive to expect these new technologies of information and renewable energy in themselves, while necessary, to be sufficient to free labor time on an equitable basis nationally, much less globally; this is critical challenge for national and transnational labor and socialist movements. The creation of this disposable time for all was seen by Marx as the necessary foundation for communism:

"The free development of individualities, and hence not the reduction of necessary labour time so as to posit surplus labour, but rather the general reduction of the necessary labour of society to a minimum, which then corresponds to the artistic, scientific etc. development of the individuals in the time set free, and with the means created, for all of them." (Marx, 1973, 706))

Gorz has followed up Marx's insights in his conception of socialism (his coquetry with using the term "communism" was surely political expediency): "A new utopia is needed if we are to safeguard what the ethical content of the socialist utopia provided; the utopia of a society of free time. The emancipation of individuals, their full development, the restructuring of society, are all to be achieved through the liberation from work. A reduction in working hours will allow individuals to discover a new sense of security, a new distancing from the 'necessities of life' and a form of existential autonomy which will encourage them to demand more autonomy within their work, political control of its objectives and a social space in which they can engage in voluntary and self-organized activities" (Gorz, 1989, 101.)

Gorz sees this struggle for emancipation as central in contemporary capitalism, increasingly incapable of providing full-time employment for all able-bodied workers. This critique has clearly influenced the program of the European greens (e.g., campaign for a basic income; see Van Parijs, 1991).

5. The Transition

Socialist transition: this of course is the immense challenge now facing all who see this world with unfettered capital as an unacceptable reality and are not satisfied with patchwork reforms. The political economic obstacles to realizing the potential of information/renewable energy technology are formidable to say the least. While technocratic projections of Worldwatch (see Luke, 1994) are highly optimistic, the power of transnationals and nation states desiring to prolong global dependence on fossil fuels should not be underestimated. Likewise, plausible scenarios of continued neocolonial subjugation of the "south" under the rubric of promoting solar energy are conceivable (e.g., a Saharan photovoltaic network controlled by transnationals supplying power to Europe under highly unequal arrangements of exchange). However, a path to a viable socialism is necessarily a "soft" path, with a sustainability coalition providing critical political force. While a coalition for sustainability will overlap with the coalitions for disarmament and democratic reforms, drawing in diverse class and social forces, including at times even fractions of monopoly capital (Footnote: This suggestion I am sure will infuriate the purists.), progress towards a sustainable economy objectively advances the possibility of a new socialist economy. While there are sectors of capital that may at times support parts of a sustainability program (while opposing other parts; e.g., manufacturers of computer chips, electric cars or wind turbines may bust unions, use hazardous materials poisoning their workers and polluting their communities etc.) there are powerful sectors, notably the transnational petroleum corporations, that will vigorously oppose it (witness the Gulf War; see O'Connor, 1991). Their power can only be matched by the transnational solidarity of trade unions, the green and antiimperialist/peace movements, of a level not yet achieved.

6. Conclusion

The heat death of the universe scenario of the 19th century has been resurrected as the attractor state for the global economy, a state of chaos and degradation, by Georgescu-Roegen and his followers. This conception is based on the mistaken conflation of the thermodynamic concepts of closed and isolated systems. A global economy powered by high-efficiency capture of solar energy avoids this attractor for the indefinite future. Solarization along with containment of the technosphere are material prerequisites for a global civilization realizing the Marxian concept of communism, while optimizing its relations to nature. These considerations should inform a viable ecosocialist movement.

*My son Peter Schwartzman helped me with research on solar energy, as well as reading the preliminary draft. I thank my other colleagues and editors who made critical comments on the first draft.

Department of Biology Howard University Washington, DC 20059 [E-mail: dws@scs.howard.edu]

References

o   Adabashev, I. 1966. Global Engineering. Moscow: Progress Publishers.
o   Afanasyev, V. n.d. Marxist Philosophy. Moscow: Foreign Language Publ. House.
o   Altvater, Elmar. 1993. The Future of the Market.. London: Verso.
o   _____. 1994. "Ecological and economic modalities of time and space", Ch. 4 pp. 76-90 in Is Capitalism Sustainable?, ed. M. O'Connor, N.Y.: Guilford Press.
o   Arrow, Kenneth J. 1981. in Energy, Economics, and the Environment. ed. Herman E. Daly and Alvaro F. Umana, AAAS Selected Symposium 64, Boulder, Colorado: Westview Press.
o   Ayres, Robert U. 1993. "Cowboys, cornucopians and long-run sustainability". Ecological Economics 8, 189-207.
o   Bailes, Kendall E. 1990. Science and Russian Culture in an Age of Revolutions. V.I. Vernadsky and His Scientific School, 1863-1945. Bloomington: Indiana University Press.
o   Barrow, John D. 1994. The Origin of the Universe. N.Y.: Basic Books.
o   _____. and Frank J. Tipler. 1988. The Anthropic Cosmological Principle. N.Y.: Oxford University Press.
o   Bernal, J.D. 1959. World Without War. N.Y.: Prometheus Books.
o   Bertalanffy, Ludwig von. 1968. General System Theory. N.Y.: George Braziller.
o   Bianciardi, C., Tiezzi, E. and S. Ulgiati. 1993. "Complete recycling of matter in the frameworks of physics, biology and ecological economics", Ecological Economics 8, 1-5.
o   Botkin, Daniel B. 1990. Discordant Harmonies. New York: Oxford University Press.
o   Boucher, Doug, Barclay, Bill, Lichtenberg, Erik, Middendorf, George, and David Schwartzman. 1993."Review of For the Common Good". Capitalism Nature Socialism 4 :3, 129-135.
o   Boyle, S. 1994. "Toward a fossil free future: The technical and economic feasibility of phasing out global fossil fuel use". Pp.353-378, in Integrative Assessment of Mitigation, Impacts, and Adaptation to Climate Change, CP-94-9, ed. N. Nakicenovic, W.D. Nordhaus, R. Richels and F.L. Toth, Laxenberg, Austria: International Institute for Applied Systems Analysis.
o   Burkett, Paul. 1996. Some ecological implications of Marx's critique of political economy.
o   Cardwell, D.S.L. 1989 (1971). From Watt to Clausius. Ames, Iowa: Iowa State University Press.

o   Commoner, Barry. 1976. The Poverty of Power. New York: Alfred A. Knopf.
o   _____. 1990. Making Peace with the Planet.. N.Y.: Pantheon.

o   Coveney, Peter and Roger Highfield. 1990. The Arrow of Time. New York: Fawcett Columbine.
o   Daly, Herman E. 1991. Steady-State Economics. 2nd edition. Washington, DC: Island Press.
o   _____. 1992. "Comment. Is the entropy law relevant to the economics of natural resource scarcity?- yes, of course it is!" Journal of Environmental Economics and Management 23, 91-95
o   _____. 1995. "Reply to Mark Sagoff's "Carrying capacity and ecological economics"", BioScience 45, 621-624.
o   _____. and John B. Cobb, Jr. 1989. For the Common Good. Boston: Beacon Press.
o   _____. and Alvaro F. Umana (editors). 1981. Energy, Economics, and the Environment. AAAS Selected Symposium 64, Boulder, Colorado: Westview Press.
o   Davies, P.C.W. 1977. The Physics of Time Asymmetry. Berkeley, California: University of California Press.
o   Doyal, Len and Ian Gough. 1991. A Theory of Human Need. N.Y.: Guilford Press.
o   Dryzek, John S. 1994. "Ecology and discursive democracy: beyond liberal capitalism and the administrative state", Ch. 9, pp. 176-197 in Is Capitalism Sustainable?, ed. M. O'Connor, New York: Guilford Press.
o   Dyke, Charles. 1988. The Evolutionary Dynamics of Complex Systems. New York: Oxford University Press.
o   Engels, Frederick. 1987. Karl Marx, Frederick Engels, Collected Work. Vol. 25. New York: International Publishers.
o   Faber, M. Niemes, H. and G. Stephan. 1987. Entropy, Environment and Resources. Berlin: Springer-Verlag.
o   Feshbach, Murray and Alfred Friendly, Jr. 1992. Ecocide in the USSR. New York: Basic Books.
o   Ford, Kenneth W., Gene I. Rocklin and Robert H. Scolow (eds.). 1975. Efficient Use of Energy, Part I - A Physics Perspective. New York: American Institute of Physics.
o   Frolov, Ivan T. 1984. Dictionary of Philosophy. New York: International Publishers.
o   _____. (ed.) 1989. "Marxist-Leninist understanding of the ecological problem". Pp. 8
17. in Ecological Knowledge in Perspective. Moscow: Nauka Publ.
o   Georgescu-Roegen, Nicholas. 1971. The Entropy Law and the Economic Process. Cambridge: Harvard University Press.
o   _____. 1976. Energy and Economic Myths. N.Y.: Pergamon Press.
o   _____. 1981. in Energy, Economics, and the Environment. ed.Herman E. Daly and Alvaro F. Umana, AAAS Selected Symposium 64, Boulder, Colorado: Westview Press.
o   _____. 1989. Afterword, in Rifkin, Jeremy, Entropy. Revised edition. New York: Bantam Books.
o   Golob, Richard and Eric Brus. 1993. The Almanac of Renewable Energy. New York: Henry Holt.
o   Gore, Al. 1992. Earth in the Balance. Boston: Houghton Mifflin.

o   Gorz, Andre. 1989. Critique of Economic Reason. London: Verso.

o   Graham, Loren R., 1987, Science, Philosophy and Human Behavior in the Soviet Union. New York: Columbia University Press.

o   Haavelmo, Trygve and Stein Hansen. 1992. "On the strategy of trying to reduce economic inequality by expanding the scale of human activity". Pp. 38-51, in Population, Technology and Lifestyle. ed. Robert Goodland, Herman E. Daly and Salah El Serafy, Washington, DC: Island Press.

o   Haeckel, Ernst. 1900. The Riddle of the Universe. N.Y.: Harper & Row.

o   Jacobs, Michael. 1991. The Green Economy. London: Pluto Press.

o   Kamshilov, Mikhail M. 1976. Evolution of the Biosphere. Moscow: Mir Publishers.

o   Kellogg, William W. 1978. "Global influences of mankind on the climate". Pp. 205-227, in Climatic Change, ed. John Gribbin, Cambridge: Cambridge University Press.

o   Kropotkin, Peter. 1989 (1902). Mutual Aid. Montreal: Black Rose Books.

o   Kuwano, Yukinori. 1994. "The PV era is coming- the way to GENESIS", Solar Energy Materials and Solar Cells 34, 27-39.

o   Kuznetsov, Boris G. 1977. Philosophy of Optimism. Moscow: Progress Publishers.

o   Lehninger, Albert L. 1965. Bioenergetics New York: W.A. Benjamin.

o   Levins, Richard and Richard Lewontin. 1985. The Dialectical Biologist. Cambridge: Harvard University Press.

o   Lovejoy, Derek. 1996. Limits to Growth? this issue.

o   Luke, Timothy W. 1994. "Worldwatching at the limits of growth", Capitalism Nature Socialism 5:2, 43-63.

o   Martinez-Alier, Juan. 1987. Ecological Economics. Cambridge, Massachusetts: Basil Blackwell.

o   Marx, Karl. 1973. Grundrisse. N.Y: Vintage Books.

o   Marx, Karl. and Frederick Engels. 1947. The German Ideology. New York: International Publishers.

o   Morowitz, Harold J. 1986. Mayonnaise and the Origin of Life. New York: Berkley.

o   O'Connor, James, 1988. "Capitalism, Nature, Socialism. A Theoretical Introduction", Capitalism Nature Socialism 1, 11-38.

o   _____. 1991. "Murder on the Orient Express: political economy of the Gulf War", Capitalism Nature Socialism 2: 2, 1-17.

o   O'Connor, Martin. 1991. "Entropy, structure, and organisational change", Ecol. Econ. 3,95-122.

o   Pimentel, David, Rodrigues, G., Wang, T., Abrams, R., Goldberg, K., Staecker, H., Ma, E., Brueckner, L., Trovato, L., Chow, C., Govindarajulu, U., and S. Boerke. 1994. "Renewable Energy: Economic and Environmental Issues". BioScience 44, 8, 536-547.

o   Prigogine, Ilya and Isabelle Stengers. 1984. Order out of Chaos. Toronto: Bantom Books.

o   Proops, J.L.R. 1987. "Entropy, information and confusion in the social sciences", Journal of Interdisciplinary Economics 1, 225-242.

o   Rifkin, Jeremy. 1980. Entropy. New York: Viking Press.

o   _____. 1989. Entropy. Revised edition. New York: Bantam Books.

o   Rothman, Tony. 1989. Science a la Mode. Princeton, New Jersey: Princeton University Press.

o   Sagoff, Mark. 1995. "Carrying capacity and ecological economics", BioScience 45, 610-620.

o   Schwartzman, David W. 1995. "Review of Vaclav Smil, Global Ecology", Quarterly Review of Biology 70:2, 239-241.
o   Schwartzman, David, Shore, Steven, Volk, Tyler, and Mark McMenamin. 1994. Self-organization of the Earth's biosphere- geochemical or geophysiological?, Origins of Life 24, 435-450.
o   Sen, Amartya. 1994. "Population: Delusion and Reality", The New York Review of Books, September 22, 62-71.
o   Smil, Vaclav. 1992. General Energetics. New York: Wiley .
o   Soleri, Paolo. 1969. Arcology: the City in the Image of Man. Cambridge, Massachusetts: MIT Press.
o   Stone, Jack L. 1993. "Photovoltaics: unlimited electrical energy from the sun", Physics Today 46:9, 22-29.
o   Taylor, Theodore B., and Charles C. Humpstone. 1973. The Restoration of the Earth.. New York: Harper Row.
o   The Scientist. 1994. September 19 news item, 9.
o   Van Parijs, Philippe. 1991. "Basic income: a green strategy for the new Europe". Pp.166-176, in Green Light on Europe. ed. Sara Parkin, London: Heretic Books.
o   Vernadsky, W.I. 1945. "The Biosphere and the noosphere", American Scientist 33, 1-12.

Part Three: The U.S. and the World

Pushing For Starvation at Home and War Abroad: A Time To Resist

By Harry Targ

Marge Piercy wrote poetically in a recent issue of *Monthly Review*, Who has little, let them have less. "The hatred of the poor, is it guilt gone rancid? That the rich have so much and still conspire to steal a baby's medicine, a woman's life, a man's heart and kidney....If they could push a button, if they could war on the poor here at home as they do abroad directly with bombs instead of legislation, think they'd hesitate?"

Robert Reich has been a visible observer of the "war on poor and working families". Recently, he extrapolated from his new film the claim that the "war" has been prosecuted across seven political fronts.

First, politicians in both state and national governments have opposed extending unemployment benefits for those who have experienced joblessness for long periods of time.

Second, these same politicians oppose raising the minimum wage.

Third, in several states governors have rejected federal resources to support Medicaid expansion under the Affordable Care Act.

Fourth, Republicans, with some Democratic co-conspirators, have passed legislation (signed by the President) to cut food stamp payments.

Fifth, at the federal level the Congress has been unable to make decisions to invest in education and expanded job training programs,

Sixth, in addition, Congress has rejected proposals to invest in rebuilding the American infrastructure (roads, bridges, transportation facilities, and green energy manufacturing).

Finally, in Red states and Congress there has been a sustained campaign to destroy the labor movement. After a thirty year attack on unions in the private sector, Congress, Red States (and in some cities like Chicago) campaigns are underway to destroy public sector unions.

Concerning United States imperialism, peace forces have won some significant victories over the last year that are in the process of being reversed. Growing pressures on the Obama administration to expand military support to Israel and/or to engage Iran militarily were defeated last summer by popular pressures and sectors of the administration who urged the use of diplomatic rather than military tools to expand the U.S. empire.

Shifting toward his neo-conservative and humanitarian interventionist advisors for a time, Obama flirted with the idea of direct military engagement against Syria. A war-weary nation, an energized peace movement, and Congressional objection forced Obama away from the war path in the Middle East. Tilting again to diplomacy the President launched, with the help of Russia, negotiations for tension reduction with Iran, the reduction of chemical weapons in Syria, and dialogue to end the brutal civil war in Syria.

War Factions Regain Initiative

However, over the last several months, the war factions in the Obama administration have regained the initiative to stifle ongoing negotiations with enemies in the Middle East in conjunction with Russia as a partner. United States covert intervention has fueled escalating protest and violence in Ukraine. Protesters demanding democratization and an end to corruption there have been superseded in their political influence by rightwing Ukrainian factions supported by United States covert operations.

U.S. intervention, clearly tied to neoconservative foreign policy influentials, led to the ouster of the corrupt but elected leader of Ukraine. Russia, fearful of the historic drive of western militarists, from the Russian civil war to Germany in two world wars, to NATO and the United States during the Cold War, moved to solidify its control of the Crimean section of Ukraine, with apparent mass support from citizens of that land. Thus began an escalation of a new Cold War which Stephen Cohen suggests has the makings of a Cuban Missile Crisis-style escalation of tensions between east and west.

With the eyes of Europe and the United States on the deepening crisis in Ukraine, United States operatives have been ratcheting up protest activities in Venezuela. Protests communicated in the U.S. media suggest massive opposition to the Venezuelan government which is framed as autocratic, driving the economy into enormous inflation, and making basic food increasingly scarce. Of course, reports on the ground suggest that protests are largely in wealthy neighborhoods, involve college students who see their economic futures as tied to the maintenance of great disparities of wealth and poverty, and reflect the traditional Latin American ruling classes' hatred of the poor. In the majority of locations in Venezuela as reflected in the geography of protest in that country and recent elections, the majority of the population passionately supports the Bolivarian Revolution.

But the National Endowment for Democracy and its various arms in both political parties and other covert agencies decided that the rightwing Venezuelans cannot oust the Chavistas through elections and must move to a new level of protest violence. For those of us with a long memory the phases of destabilization in Venezuela can be referred to with five letters, CHILE.

What is behind the escalating and ruthless rejection of minimally humane policies in the many states and the country at large as listed by Reich? And what is behind the escalation to war overseas, with the clear goal of ending any chance of negotiating settlements of violent disputes, reversing Russia's (and later China's) influence in the world, and destroying people's movements in Latin America?

The American Legislative Exchange Council (ALEC) and the Theory of the 'Deep State'

ALEC was founded in 1973 by Paul Weyrich and noted conservatives such as Senator Jesse Helms and John Kasich to raise money and coordinate the creation of a counter-revolution in the American political system. Its vision was one of deregulation, privatization, weakening workers' rights, and the facilitation of the unbridled accumulation of private wealth. The achievement of these goals required the rejection of the public commitment to positive government; the idea that for societies to function, public energies, resources, and commitments are needed to create and maintain institutions to serve the people. This is so whether the topic of concern is national security, public safety, education and infrastructure, and/or providing for the needy.

ALEC established a network of prominent politicians at the national and state levels, created well-funded lobby groups, funded "research" to justify reactionary public policies, supported conservative political candidates running for office virtually everywhere and at all levels of government. ALEC creates "model" legislation that is introduced in legislative bodies everywhere on subjects like right-to-work, charter schools, and privatization of pensions. While politicians pay dues to join ALEC, over 98 percent of ALEC's budget comes from corporate contributions from such economic and political influentials as Exxon/Mobil, the Koch brothers, the Coors family, and the Scaife family. ALEC claims to have 2,000 legislative members and over 300 corporate members. Corporations who have benefited legislatively from their affiliations with ALEC include but are not limited to Altria/Philip Morris USA, Humana, United Healthcare, Corrections Corporation of America, and Connections Academy.

One of ALEC's prominent projects is the creation of the "State Policy Network," a collection of think tanks in every state (funded up to $83 million) to generate research "findings" to justify the rightwing model legislation generated by ALEC. SPN studies have been disseminated on education healthcare, worker's rights, energy and the environment, taxes, government spending, and wages and income equality (Center For Media and Democracy, "Exposed: The State Policy Network," November, 2013, p.6).

Of particular concern to workers are the ALEC model bills that have been introduced in states attacking workers. These include:

· right-to-work legislation
· rules increasing the right for governments to hire non-union contractors
· changing pension rights for government employees
· repealing minimum wage laws
· eliminating prevailing wage laws for construction workers
· encouraging so-called "free trade" to outsource work
· privatizing public services
· gutting worker's compensation

The role of ALEC, the Koch Brothers, and the largest multinational corporations and banks in America suggest that politics increasingly occurs at two levels. First, at the level of transparency, we observe politics as "games," largely about electoral contests, gossip and frivolous rhetoric. News junkies avidly consume this first level, glued to the television screen or the social network.

However, Mike Lofgren, a former Republican Congressional aid has introduced the idea of another level of politics, what he calls the "deep state." Lofgren defines the "deep state" as "... a hybrid association of elements of government and parts of top-level finance and industry that is effectively able to govern in the United States without reference to the consent of the governed as expressed through the formal political process." (Mike Lofgren, "Anatomy of the 'Deep State': Hiding in Plain Sight," Online University of the Left, February 23, 2014). Others have examined invisible power structures that rule America (from C. W. Mills' classic *The Power Elite*, Oxford University Press, 2000, to Robert Perrucci, Earl Wysong, and David Wright, *The New Class Society: Goodbye American Dream?* Rowman and Littlefield, 2013).

The distinction between politics as games vs. the deep state suggest that the power to make critical decisions resides not in the superstructure of the political process; the place where competitive games are played for all to see, but in powerful institutions embedded in society that can make decisions without requiring popular approval. In domestic politics, the "deep state" apparatuses such as ALEC and its network of organizational ties has initiated a resource-rich campaign – from the school board and city council to the state and nation – to destroy the links between government and the people. Recall Marge Piercy's reference to "war on the poor." And the public face of the deep state includes the selective and manipulative character of experts, pundits, and major sources of news in the media. This includes what news consumers are told and what they are not told.

The 'Deep State' and Foreign Policy

Journalist Robert Parry has recently described the character of the "deep state" and patterns of interference in Ukraine (Robert Perry, "A Shadow US Foreign Policy," consortium news. com, February 27, 2014). Funding for covert operations in support of "democratization" was initiated by Congress in 1983 when it established the National Endowment for Democracy. NED currently receives $100 million a year to engage in non-transparent activities such as in Venezuela and Ukraine.

Parry raises the issue of who is controlling U.S. covert operations: "NED is one reason why there is so much confusion about the administration's policies toward attempted ousters of democratically elected leaders in Ukraine and Venezuela. Some of the non-government organizations (or NGOs) supporting these rebellions trace back to NED and its U.S. government money, even as Secretary of State John Kerry and other senior officials insist the U.S. is not behind these insurrections."

As a result of ousted President Yanukovych's turn away from joining the European Union, which would require Ukraine to accept IMF/EU austerity policies, the deep state institutions shifted from supporting the elected Ukraine president to funding various opposition elements to him.

Parry reports that Carl Gershman, neoconservative and president of NED wrote in the Washington Post last September that the U.S. should push all the countries in Central Europe to accept so-called free trade agreements and the neoliberal policy agenda. Although the long-term goal would be removing Putin from office, Parry said that NED has funded 65 projects in Ukraine creating a "shadow political structure of media and activist groups." According to Gershman, "Ukraine is the biggest prize." It is likely that much more data will be uncovered in the weeks ahead (primarily in alternative media) about United States involvement in Ukraine, Venezuela, and the dozens of other countries in which the deep structures of the national security apparatus operate. For now, several points can be made:

First, a multiplicity of agencies, bureaus, funded organizations (often called non-governmental organizations or NGOs) engage in semi-independent foreign policies with political groups in other countries. In addition, banks, multinational corporations, so-called human rights organizations and other NGOs are part of the panoply of interventionist organizations that promote an imperial agenda.

Second, it is not always clear that deep state structures reflect the official foreign policies defined by the President or members of the National Security Council who are supposed to be the public face of United States foreign policy to the world and the American people.

Third, these deep structures promote long discredited foreign policies that have their roots in the post-World War Two period or even further, the Russian Revolution (when the United States and 9 other countries sent troops to help the counter-revolutionaries in their effort to overthrow the new government established by the Bolsheviks).

Fourth, these deep structures also promote the neoliberal policy agenda across the global economy: privatization of public institutions, so-called "free markets," cutting government services so that countries can pay back loans from international financial institutions, export development policies, and disempowering workers, peasants, those barely surviving in the informal sector.

Fifth, even if the President and key foreign policy decision-makers are not in control of the deep state they still bear responsibility for the correction of policies created by it.

The Moral Mondays Fightback

The most exciting social movement development occurring over the last two years is in the South. In North Carolina the determined, passionate, and constant protest against a reactionary Koch Brothers-like legislative agenda has brought thousands of activists to the state capital in Raleigh for almost a year. Throughout the spring legislative session activists have engaged in civil disobedience, leading by last June to over 1,000 arrests.

The leadership of Moral Mondays includes Rev. William Barber who has argued that we are in the midst of the "third reconstruction." The first reconstruction, after the Civil War consisted of Black and white workers who struggled to create a democratic South (which would have impacted on the North as well). It was crushed by white racism and the estab-lishment of Jim Crow segregation. The second reconstruction occurred between Brown vs. Board of Education in 1954 and candidate Nixon's "Southern strategy." During this period segregation was overturned, Medicare and Medicaid were established, and Social Security was ex-panded. Blacks and whites benefited.

Now we are in the midst of a third reconstruction. Twenty-first century struggles are based on "fusion" politics; that is bringing all activists – Black, Brown, white, gay/straight, environmentalists—together. Fusion politics assumes that only a mass movement built on everyone's issues can challenge the Koch brothers numerically. Also, each issue is inter-connected causally with every other issue.

Moral Mondays has been gaining more and more visibility; from North Carolina to South Carolina, Georgia, Florida, soon Arizona, and up to the Midwest. The movement is based on organizational pragmatism and leadership, a multi-dimensional fightback strategy, and fusion of class, race, and gender.

Building a Better Political Future: Fightbacks, Fusion Politics, Intersectionality, and Moving Beyond Finance Capitalism

The growing economic devastation and political marginalization of the working class broadly defined is the centerpiece of the crisis of our age. At base, the profit system, competition and capital accumulation, the appropriation of the value of all goods and services by corporations and banks, political systems that inevitably reflect the needs and interests of the economically powerful, dramatically constrict the capacity to create a humane society, one where the maximization of human possibility is achieved. The analyses of the U.S. economy and polity at this time raise fundamental questions of how to resist, fightback, and create the pos-sibility of a better world.

Tentative answers to the fundamental question of how to achieve signifi-cant social change requires a sober assessment of where we are today.

What are the basic parameters of economic life in the nation and the community? Who governs our political institutions? What are the realistic forces of resistance? What are the relative merits--given power, skill, numbers of people, levels of organization and traditional values--of electoral work, mass mobilizations, and constructing alternative institutions in the intersections of existing society?

Six general points can be raised now:

First, given the varied attacks, as articulated by Robert Reich, on wages and income, on jobs, on healthcare, on education, on transportation, reproductive rights, and basic environmental survivability, fightback movements are justified on all fronts. The assault on the vast majority of humankind occurs in multiple areas, in multiple ways, and across policy areas.

Second, as opposed to the capacity to mobilize masses of people around single issues – the right to form unions, anti-racism, peace – in the twentieth century, twenty-first century movements require what Reverend William Barber calls "fusion" politics. Grassroots and national campaigns around single issues need to be cognizant of and connect with the multiplicity of issues that shape human concern. Twenty first century movements should be built on the proposition that these struggles are inextricably connected.

Third, it has become clear today that what the great progressive movements of the past knew intuitively but not theoretically is that the intersection of class, race, gender, and environmental consciousness constructs our problems and how we are going to resolve them. Workers, people of color, and women, with different gender preferences and concerns about the physical survival of the planet are all in the same fight and must recognize it.

Fourth, in countries that have long traditions and institutions that regularize political competition, particularly elections, it is necessary to recognize that for lots of people those institutions matter. In the United States when most people talk about "politics" they are talking about elections. And as we see in critical moments in our history, elections matter. But, at the same time, the electoral arena is very much affected by unconventional politics: mass mobilizations, protest rallies, civil disobedience, shop floor and beer hall conversations and even threats of violence. The history of social change in America confirms that these kinds of politics matter and matter profoundly. These assumptions lead to the proposition that the politics of reform and revolution require "inside" and "outside" strategies, often at the same time. And recent history suggests that the power of money which increasingly has shaped inside strategy usually can only be challenged by the mobilization of people, the outside strategy.

Fifth, while social movements have always been international, given twenty-first century technology they are increasingly so. Paul Robeson, W. E. B. Dubois, George Padmore informed worldwide audiences about the great movements to destroy the colonial systems in Africa and Asia. These struggles also informed and inspired struggles for liberation in the United States as well. In our own day, Arab Spring, mobilizations of workers in the Heartland of the United States, occupy movements, student protests in Quebec and Santiago, the Bolivarian Revolution, and open rebellion in Greece and Spain were increasingly seen as part of the same struggle for human liberation. Now, a modest protest in one geographic space somewhere in the world becomes a global event within a matter of hours. And the concerns are often the same even if the historical contexts vary. The old IWW adage, "an injury to one is an injury to all," for reasons of the new technology has been transformed from a slogan to a reality.

Finally, often what animates a movement is the embrace of an issue: access to healthcare, raising the minimum wage, ending hydro fracking, eliminating racist laws, opposing military interventionism. And, as we return to our own communities, we see that what gets people motivated to act is often that single issue that most immediately affects them. From there, the job of progressives is to promote fusion politics; highlight its relevance to class, race, and gender; develop inside/outside strategies to fight back; and to connect grassroots struggles to national and international struggles.

The specifics of this are terribly difficult but the basic outlines are clear. Now we need to act.

Shifting to Balanced and Sustainable Development: A Brief Overview of China's 2013 Communist Party Central Committee Plenum

By Duncan McFarland
CCDS Peace and Solidarity Committee

China watchers in 2013 focused on the Communist Party central committee plenum in November, where the new leadership detailed the national socio-economic development plan through 2020. This was the first opportunity for the new General Secretary Xi Jinping and Premier Li Keqiang to detail their policy direction. Grabbing the headlines inthe Western press is the loosening of China's one child policy; nowmany urban couples will have a second child.   Another headline wasChina's decision to abolish *laojiao*, the system of re-education through labor.

The meeting created two new high-level bodies: a Chinese national securitycouncil to coordinate military and diplomatic strategy, and a reform oversight group to coordinate domestic economic and political structurechanges.   These committees will strengthen the hand of GeneralSecretary Xi, who is emerging as a more forceful leader than hislower profile predecessor, Hu Jintao.   China's subsequent declaration of an Air Defense Identification Zone over adjacent space over the East China Seacorroborates this impression.

Regarding economics, China is shifting from a capital-intensive, export-driven, fast growth model to a balanced and sustainable domestic development program, featuring rising incomes, expanded social services and concern for the environment and pollution. This is considered a major turning point in socialist China's development as the Deng Xiaoping rapid industrialization and modernization program adopted in Dec. 1978 has achieved most of its goals. It is now urgent to deal with the attendant problems of great concern to the Chinese people: the wide income gap between the newly affluent and most working people, serious environmental damage and pollution, and official corruption. The new leadership seeks to address these problems as a top priority.

General Secretary Xi's political approach is to emphasize Leninist institutions such as the leading role of the Communist Party, the importance of Marxist ideology and the necessity of state ownership andcontrol of strategic economic sectors such as the financial system and important heavy industry. State provided social services will be expanded and resourced with more funds. At the same time, Xi favors the continued development of the economic reform program with increased opening to market forces and strengthening of the non-public sector. Some Western observers see this as a contradiction; Xi appears as a "conservative" traditional Marxist in politics while favoring a liberal economic program.

China describes its mixed economy model as a socialist market economy. There is both a socialist sector with state and collective property, and a "nonpublic" or capitalistic sector -- roughly equal in size. The Communist Party retains political and macroeconomic control and is guiding the country towards socialism in the long term. While this approach was pioneered by the Soviet Union in the 1920's as the New Economic Policy (NEP), China has gone much further down this road and is now entering a new phase of development, historically unprecedented.

The challenge is colossal. The theory of the mixed economy is clear:Communist Party control of the strategic sectors such as the financial system and major industry is combined with expansion of the private market and foreign invested enterprises. This approach is appropriate for socialist development in a developing country building a modern economy. However, getting the practical policies right in a huge, complex ancient country like China, emerging from 2000 years of feudalism, is difficult indeed.

Deep Contradictions

There are many profound contradictions and dilemmas in addition to the tension between socialism and capitalism: high technology vs. persistent primitive agricultural methods; city and countryside; the central government balancing with powerful provincial and local interests; the advanced coastal cities and international markets and the vast more backward interior; the state and civil society; the livelihood of the people vs. capital accumulation. Only experience an provide answers to many of the emerging problems.

Financial policies and structures are high on the 3rd plenum agenda: government revenues, taxation, transparent budgeting, prices, currency valuation, attracting and controlling foreign investment, stock market-regulations, creating more small banks, regulating interest rates and-paying increased dividends. The tasks of managing state owned enterprises are different than those of regulating the nonpublic or private economy; meanwhile, more and more mixed ownership arrangements combining public and private are created.

The 3rd plenum plan also contains many measures for social justice and equality: strengthening trade unions and support for collective bargaining; increasing farmers' incomes; extending social services to migrant workers; supporting local direct elections, consultation and grassroots democracy; various ways to expand financing of the social security system; easing restrictions of movement for those wanting to move the small and medium sized cities; substantial penalties for enterprises violating environmental regulations. There is a major emphasis on supporting cultural institutions of all sorts.

Conclusion

The Chinese people welcome the balanced, people-centered program of the new leadership. However, there are powerful obstacles such as both traditional semi-feudal forces working with new capitalist and foreign capitalists. There is no guarantee of success or prevention of a capitalist restoration. Are there ways that we may evaluate the success of the 3rd plenum program? While the battle against official corruption is difficult for foreigners to evaluate, improvements in the environment and narrowing of the income gap should be visible. Increasing living standards of migrant workers and Chinese people, and poverty alleviation are apparent. State macroeconomic control and retention of control of the "commanding heights" of the economy (such as continued state ownership of the banks) will be necessary to ensure socialist economic and social development.

The Rightist Threat in Europe
- And the Left

By Victor Grossman

Will rightists, racists and other rabble gain new
strength with the elections to the European
Union? And does it matter if they do? The first
answer should be known by the time you read
this. The second question raises a tangle of new
questions hotly debated in left-wing circles all
around Europe.

The European Union is viewed by its advocates,
sometimes dreamily, as a way towards a United
States of Europe, forever ending the long, bitter
history of rivalries and wars on this complicated
continent. Others, on the right and on the left,
pour cold water on the dreamers, reject support
for the EU, and even urge its dissolution - for totally different reasons.

Two men are generally honored as EU founders. The conservative Robert Schuman, briefly a minister in Marshall Petain's fascist government
in 1940, spent most of the war in a monastery, perhaps praying but
also hatching plans for Europe. In 1950, as French Foreign Minister, he
made a famous speech which set the unifying machinery in motion. Jean
Monnet, a leading French advocate of European unity, probably wrote
the speech. Rarely noted are two other main players: Winston Churchill,
hoping to smother any left leanings of the Labor government which replaced him and still eager to play a major role in the world, and Konrad
Adenauer, seeking respectability for the West German republic, whose
first Chancellor he had become in 1949.

But, delving deeper, one finds the American Committee on a United Europe (ACUE), organized in 1948 by William Donovan, boss of the wartime
Office of Strategic Services (OSS), and by Allen Dulles, soon to head its
successor, the Central Intelligence Agency (CIA). Presidents Truman and
Eisenhower believed that European unification would help overcome post-
war anti-German feelings, especially in France, easing acceptance of West
Germany as a political, economic and military base for overcoming leftist
influence in Western Europe and weakening the position of the USSR.

Using this ACUE, the US government secretly contributed millions of dollars to support the Schuman Plan, integrating French and German coal and steel industries and forming the base of the European Union. The Rockefeller and Ford foundations were also financially very generous. Churchill, the vital link between ACUE and Europeans, saw in this "unofficial counterpart" of the Marshall Plan, the "liberation of the nations behind the Iron Curtain" and a path to "our aim and ideal, nothing less than the union of Europe as a whole."

The goal was never abandoned. Key remnants of the USSR have been partly or fully integrated into the EU or NATO: the Baltic States, Georgia, and Azerbaijan. US crusaders lead their European junior partners in a charge to win the potentially wealthy, strategically crucial Ukraine, almost closing the ring in their steady advance eastward - with the final goal at the Moskva River. This, a main purpose of the EU, has at this writing achieved control at least of Kiev and the Western Ukraine.

But the EU also plays a questionable role in other ways. Angela Merkel's "austerity" policy, in line with the big banks and a rigid euro, has brought frightening economic disaster to much of southern Europe. EU policies on keeping asylum-seekers and the economically desperate from European shores, backed by the European Council's naval-military Frontex units, cause countless deaths in stormy Mediterranean waters. EU and US business men are secretly engaged in bridging the Atlantic with a planned trade treaty which would permit an unhindered import to Europe of biotic-stuffed and gene-manipulated foods, lower safety standards, worse working conditions plus an increase in the deluge of Hollywood films, paperback trivia, intellectual patent limitations and similar blessings. Finally, the EU is building up a military force which, with the NATO, spreads its will to all continents. Approaches to socialism on any continent would certainly be squelched.

With such a background and such policies, why should any leftist group have anything to do with it or its elections? Indeed, some reply sharply: "It shouldn't!"

But the matter is complicated - like the structure of the EU, which consists of six different bodies. Its judicial section is in Luxembourg, its central bank in Frankfurt and most governing bodies in Brussels, including a sort of Upper House and the European Council, where heads of states meet four times a year. For its executive body, the European Commission, each of the 28 member states nominates one commissioner, who is assigned a different ministry and portfolio. These write a host of binding rules and regulations: on subsidies for aiding depressed areas, pushing or discouraging certain crops, on smog, gene-manipulated foods, consumer standards, human rights and much more.

Currently being elected is the European Parliament (EP), which commutes between Brussels and its main home in French Strasbourg, across the Rhine from Germany. It is, since 1979, the only EU body elected by nearly 500 million Europeans. The 751 members, seated for five years, are apportioned more or less by population. Germans can vote for 96 delegates, France 74 and Italy and Britain 73 each. A minimum of six each is allotted to little Malta, Luxembourg, Estonia and Cyprus. Since they make speeches in their own languages, a giant, expensive team of translators is needed.

This Parliament, once hardly more than an appendix, has gradually gained weight and influence. Here is where political battles are fought, with members dividing not by nation but usually by political caucus, from left to right. Over the years the EP has won the right to disapprove of commissioners (not individually but only "all or none"). It succeeded in barring a nastily homophobic Italian politician from a commission, forcing a reshuffling. And while this EP cannot initiate legislation as yet, it can make proposals and must grant its approval.

Despite its many conservative members there have been good decisions, partly because public pressure on this EP is at least possible. They have included improvements in standards of consumer goods and the rights of working people, hindering attempts to increase the length of the working week and restrict the right to strike. The EP helped prevent the European Commission in Brussels from a retreat on privatizing water rights, it pushed the commissioners into acting against foodstuff speculation, especially with baby foods, and is engaged in hot controversy on opening the secret negotiations on the transatlantic Free Trade pact to public view.

In many investigations on human rights issues it has taken varied positions, not always what leftists would want, but sometimes vigorous in criticizing violations, including a "denunciation of criminal conduct" by both sides in Syria, a sharp review on the denial of human rights in Bahrain and a demand that Israel end its mistreatment of Palestinian prisoners, especially women and children, often for many years without trial, legal counsel or family visits. Such resolutions, though not binding, can be very useful in winning Europe-wide publicity.

Such possibilities offer one argument for leftists to accept the EU as a fact of life and work within it, making the best of every opportunity. There is another argument: the alarming growth of rightist parties and movements, some very extreme, which hope, by increasing their representation, to either destroy the institution and revert to nationalist, chauvinist action on a state by state basis, or to use the EP to gain publicity, win prestige and move closer to extreme right-wing if not fascist power. The economic crisis of 2007-2008, still causing havoc, and results of any new crisis, open the way for such a growing danger. This can best be shown on a country by country rundown.

France

The biggest headlines of the elections on May 22-25 could well be grabbed by the French Front National (FN) if it wins most or almost most of the 74 seats allotted to France. It now challenges both Francois Hollande's Socialist Party, still in power but drastically weakened by municipal elections, and Nicolas Sarkozy's conservative MRP.

The poll results are fluid and flexible, like so much connected with FN. Its main founder, Jean-Marie Le Pen, 86, a right-wing rabble-rouser from his schooldays who just missed the chance to fight Vietnamese or at Suez the Egyptians but finally got a chance to fight as a lieutenant in Algeria where, he has admitted, "I tortured because we had to." At first, in 1972, his Front National was far-right Catholic, anti-Communist and anti-Semitic, with some monarchists and men nostalgic about one-time harmony with the Nazi occupation. Le Pen's words became notorious:

"I'm not saying the gas chambers didn't exist. I haven't seen them myself. I haven't particularly studied the question." And later: "If you take a 1000-page book on World War II, the concentration camps take up only two pages and the gas chambers 10 to 15 lines. This is what one calls a detail."

His FN called for "law and order": tougher sentences, more prisoners, and a return to the death penalty. Its nationalist, chauvinist position increasingly meant hatred of immigrants, especially those from North Africa, former West African colonies and the Near East, basically Muslims and people of color. It graciously qualified its demand for deportation: "...only criminal, illegal or unemployed aliens". The negative term "lepénisation" was born.

Such nationalism paid off in the presidential elections of 2002, when he beat the Socialist Jospin for a chance in the run-off duel against the conservative Jacques Chirac. Most people were frightened with over a million demonstrating against him during the week that followed. Even those on the Left, intensely opposed to the conservative MRP, said "Rather a crook than a fascist" and voted for Chirac, who won overwhelmingly with 82 percent, while Le Pen still got a worrisome 17.8 percent.

In 2011 Le Pen, while keeping his European seat, turned over reins in the FN to his youngest daughter Marine, 46, (born Marion Anne Le Pen). Clever, modern, intent on winning new voter groups, she announced progressive demands for health and welfare benefits, against privatization of utilities, the post offices or social security, called for restrictions on banks and fairer taxes on gas and oil profiteers. She opposed the Libyan War and dropped her father's anti-Semitic statements, hoping to win Jewish voters. But she rejected labeling all criticism of Israeli policies as "anti-Semitism" and called for an end to "West Bank" Israeli settlements. A planned visit to Israel was hindered by those who recalled FN anti-Semitism. Like her father she was sharply critical of the EU but eagerly sought more seats in its EP.

Despite positions which did not sound reactionary, she kept hammering at her constant main theme. While avoiding unreal demands that all immigrants be deported and saying only that immigration must be stopped and borders better guarded, she utilized all the right code words to intensify the fears and hates of many working people against those with a different skin color, language, religion or culture. And she knew well how to impress TV viewers.

Marine Le Pen also praised the Tea Party movement in the USA and Ron Paul, but he was careful to avoid any meeting with this contradictory but unpleasantly far, far right European.

In the presidential elections of 2012 the FN, with 17.9 percent, came in third. In recent local elections it gained in some towns, captured one borough in Marseilles but was spurned by all other parties. Yet it was largely fear of FN's strength which led President Hollande, after losing out almost everywhere to conservatives, to name a new premier who adopted many of the chauvinist, anti-Muslim, anti-Roma attitudes of the Le Pens. For the EP vote on May 25th, anything is possible.

United Kingdom

Like the French Front National, Britain's main right-wing party opposes the European Union and everything connected with it, except the financial subsidies for all parties represented. Indeed, opposing the EU is the major platform plank of the United Kingdom Independence Party (UKIP), which has largely replaced the very fascist British National Party. It refrains from thuggish BNP ways and, like the FN, tries to downplay violent tones, without abandoning its coded, "moderate" message that immigrants are problem No. 1 and should, if not thrown out altogether, be kept from any increase in number or access to public assistance. Our economic woes, says the UKIP, are the fault of foreigners, those across the Channel and those who have squeezed into "our Britain".

Its stress on quitting the EU is popular in the island kingdom, with pressure growing for a national referendum on the matter and enabling the UKIP, founded in 1993, to gain a growing membership, now about 36,000. It has never gained a seat in the House of Commons (though coming close once) but in voting for the EP, with proportional representation, it won an amazing second place, getting 13 of the UK's 73 seats. Its aim - increasingly within reach - is to beat out the Liberal Democrats, now governing with the Conservatives. In its view "the Liberal Democrats are no longer the voice of opposition in British politics - we are. Between now and the next general election our aim is to replace them as third party in British politics."

To avoid being seen as a one-theme party, UKIP adopts positions on other subjects, like support of the monarch, who must remain "Defender of the Faith", and a restoration of public oaths of allegiance to the queen. More than against anti-royalists, that is directed against non-Anglican Church members of any hue. Indeed, when Prince Charles, visiting Strasbourg in 2008, called for EU leadership on climate change, UKIP leader Nigel Farage was the only member to stay seated during the standing ovation.

This was in line with the UKIP disbelief in man-made climate change, like some in the USA. It rejects investment in renewable energy or even showing films on climate change in schools. Farage, for whom "the slight warming in the last hundred years is... consistent with long-term natural climate cycles", sees plans for wind energy as "loopy". One UKIP politician said the aim of a UN climate treaty was to "impose a communist world government". Maybe it was fears like this which caused the UKIP to call for a 40 percent increase in defense spending and the purchase of three new aircraft carriers.

After years of internal dissension, Nigel Farage, 50, is now the debonair, well-spoken head - and dictator - of the UKIP. Like Marine Le Pen, he tries to avoid sounding openly racist. During local elections in 2013 the UKIP announced that it was investigating six candidates "over links to the British National Party and other far right groups or alleged racist and homophobic comments". Some were suspended from the party and such stabs at respectability have evidently had great success.

So, too, have Farage's exposés of dirty dealings in the EU, often too well-founded, including a French designate as EU commissioner who had been barred from elected office in France for embezzling government funds but was covered by President Chirac. A leading conservative EP member had been under investigation for a far larger sum. Most sensationally, Farage charged that the president of the EU Commission, José Manuel Barroso, had spent a luxurious week on a Greek billionaire's yacht a month before the Commission approved 10.3 million euro in Greek state aid for his shipping company. Farage was clever enough to say loudly things which many people thought; he told the president of the European Council, Belgian ex-Premier Herman Van Rompuy, that he had the "charisma of a damp rag and the appearance of a low grade bank clerk" and asked him, "Who are you? I'd never heard of you, nobody in Europe had ever heard of you". But when Farage was himself accused of receiving large annual sums to run his office (although supporters provided it rent-free) he angrily called the allegations "outrageous, ridiculous and absurd".

Farage is a clever speaker who bested Nicholas Clegg, Liberal-Democratic vice-premier, in two TV duels, partly because so many charges against the government are well-founded. Yet despite his caution, candidates occasionally reveal the UKIP's main stock in trade. Contradicting a black singer's complaint about poor representation of ethnic minorities on TV, one UKIP leader tweeted: "He should emigrate to a black country. He does not have to live with whites." Another stated that "Islam reminds me of the 3rd Reich, strength through violence against the citizens" and "Muslims like us to fawn to them." A few extremists were sacrificed, like one UKIP big shot who blamed recent floods on Prime Minister Cameron because of his support of same-sex marriage.

The UKIP was awarded major party status for the European elections and allotted the same number of broadcasts as mainstream parties and "due weight" in news broadcasts. This helped it reach an alarming 18 percent, inducing Cameron, like Hollande in France, to bend to UKIP positions, in Britain mostly against people from India, Pakistan, the Near East and Eastern Europe. He does not want to lose potential right-wing votes.

Not everyone falls for the mix of slick words and nasty racism, especially not in left-leaning Scotland. At a press conference in Edinburgh, protesters interrupted Farage, accused him of being "racist", "fascist" and a "homophobe" and told him to "go back to London". When the atmosphere worsened Farage found it wise to leave in an armored police van. But it looks as if he and a large UKIP contingent may play an important role in organizing the extreme right in coming EP sessions in Strasbourg and Brussels.

Netherlands

In the Netherlands of all places, once so tolerant, an unusually bad apple can be found. He is very blond, very handsome (to some) and very active; his name is Geert Wilders and he heads a virulent party also built on hatred towards immigrants. Forced by mass imports of cheap foodstuffs and manufactured goods from developed countries into giant, miserable city ghettos and driven to desperation, people risked emigration, legal or often dangerously illegal, to seek survival in presumably wealthy

Europe and send back help to their families. They do the dirty work, the illegal work, or are jobless. The poverty and inevitable marginal crime of frequently hopeless young generations are distorted and dramatized by the mass media, clearing the way for right-wing extremists to misdirect the anger of precarious local groups - not upward against those responsible but downward against the greatest victims. In the Netherlands these were once Indonesians and Surinamese. Now they are mostly Moroccans.

The Dutch far-right movement was shaped by an unusual professor, Pym Fortuyn, whose crusade, "a cold war with Islam... an extraordinary threat, a hostile religion", won his party the Rotterdam city council in 2002, beating the Labor Party for the first time since the war. Just days before a national election which promised big gains, he was murdered in a parking lot by an angry opponent (not a Muslim). The murder shook the country but his party soon withered away.

It was Geert Wilders who then hoisted the anti-Muslim banner and founded his own fiefdom, the Party for Freedom (PVV). Just as hateful as Fortuyn, he attacks the Koran as "a fascist book" and promotes his film "Fitna", an attack on Islam in the bloodiest rabble-rousing - but very effective - tradition. His surprising 15.5 percent of the national vote in 2010 induced two center-right parties to form a minority government which relied for support on Wilders' PVV, agreeing in return to drastically cut "non-western" immigration.

When the coalition fell apart and the PVV temporarily dipped in popularity polls, Wilders expanded his hate scenario, offering a web-site for the public to "register complaints regarding job and social problems" caused by Eastern European immigrants. This led the European Parliament to pass a resolution condemning the site for fostering hate and discrimination; Wilders countered with a call to cancel the EU membership of Rumania and Bulgaria.

While polling and voting results for the PVV averaged about ten or fifteen percent, its racism infected far wider circles, and some predicted it might win most of the 26 Dutch EP seats. If so, Wilders threatened, there will be "fewer Moroccans in the Netherlands". (One PVV member, an EP delegate, was quoted saying it was "appropriate not to give water to refugees in reception camps". Five months later he lost the EP seat - because of drunken driving.)

Wilders is often seen outside Dutch borders, busy forging an extremist alliance for a "Europe of Fatherlands" instead of a "United States of Europe" - for him the "monster in Brussels". He has addressed rallies in

Berlin and the USA and raved against the proposed Muslim center near "Ground Zero" in New York City.

Austria

A majority of Austrians welcomed Hitler's take-over in 1938; a good third were actively involved in Nazi activities, making the situation different from most of Europe (except Germany), where anti-Nazi feelings ran high after the war and anti-fascist veterans played important roles. Austria liked to call itself "the first country victimized by Hitler" but both leading parties, the Austrian People's Party (ÖVP) and the Socialists (SPÖ), avoided hurting too many feelings of unreformed fascists, who also formed an openly nostalgic party, led by SS men, which placed third in 1949 elections.

This became embarrassing. It was replaced in 1955 by the Austrian Freedom Party (FPÖ), a mix of currents, some still pro-German, others definitely Austrian, but all far to the right. It hobbled along at about 5 per cent status until 1986 when, like other similar parties, it found a charismatic new leader, Jörg Haider, the governor of Carinthia province. He built up the party on the usual nationalist, anti-immigration, anti-EU feelings, showing that he had not moved far from the active Nazi past of his father, When an opponent criticized his proposal to cut unemployment aid for "freeloaders" (a code word for immigrants), calling it "reminiscent of Nazi policies" of forced labor, Haider retorted: "No, they didn't have that in the Third Reich, in the Third Reich they had a proper employment policy, which not even your government in Vienna can manage to bring about."

Such praise of Nazis was a mite too hearty, especially outside Austria; Haider had to quit as governor of Carinthia. But a third of all Austrians felt his words were factually correct; 42 percent believed criticism in the press had been exaggerated.

He soon came back, not only in Carinthia, and the FPÖ climbed to 27% in 1999 polls. A year later the leading People's Party broke its long alliance with the Social Democrats to join with Haider's Freedom Party in a coalition government, causing fourteen EU states to break official connections with Austria. But within a year they somehow swallowed their indignation and ended the boycott. In Carinthia even the Social Democrats supported this admirer of Nazi ways who, speaking to a meeting of old Nazi SS-men, said the veterans were "decent people of good character" who "remain true to their convictions."

His main line was always racism, clothed in Muslimophobia. "The social order of Islam is opposed to our Western values," he asserted. "Human rights and democracy are as incompatible with the Muslim religious doctrine as is the equality of women. In Islam, the individual and his free will count for nothing; faith and religious struggle - jihad, the holy war - for everything." Here again a feigned love of gender equality was misused for the same old attacks on a minority. His personal touch was opposition to any form of bilingualism in his state of Carinthia with its many people of Slovenian descent. He called for separation of Slovene and German children in the schools and refused to abide by a court decision for bilingual road signs in mixed neighborhoods, personally moving the sign in one town for several yards in defiance of the order.

Then, in 2008, Haider, speeding at double the legal limit and possibly alcoholized, crashed down an embankment to his death. The nearby bridge was renamed Jörg Haider Bridge for the lost hero.

But even without Haider the Freedom Party carried on successfully. The new FPÖ head, Hans-Christian Stracke, kept on against foreigners, especially Muslims, also Jews, and against the EU, which was portrayed as crooks yearning for "our" hard-won earnings. One caricature of "the bankers" - equated with the EU - was viciously anti-Semitic but OK'd if not authorized by Stracke. Posthumous scandals about Haider and his involvement in immense embezzlement dealings (with very Germanic Bavarian) bankers did not faze Stracke in the least.

Austria is small but Vienna is big and sometimes plays host to similar parties from northern and eastern Europe, aimed at forging an alliance to keep berating the EU while building strength in its Parliament. Stracke's FÖP can hope for a vote of over 20 percent - and an increased number of Austria's 18 EP members.

Greece

It's hard to decide which of the next two cases is uglier and more dangerous. Let us start with Greece. After suffering far more than its share of occupation, civil war and dictatorship, and after American, German and other bankers and weapon-makers had siphoned its wealth into their deep pockets for years with the assistance of two corrupt parties, it found itself abysmally in debt. Then the "Troika" moved in, gentlemen from the International Monetary Fund in Washington, the European Commission in Brussels, and the European Central Bank in Frankfurt (the latter two, part of the European Union). In accord with Angela Merkel's "austerity" policy they insisted on a full horror cabinet of draconian measures, ruining the remains of its economy and impoverishing huge sections of the population, with 28 percent unemployed and 60 percent of the young people largely hopeless.

One result was the growth of a strong left-wing group, later a party, called Syriza, which barely missed winning first place in national elections in 2012. All high level efforts ever since, domestic and international, have been directed toward keeping Syriza out of power.

The other result, perhaps related to this effort, was the sudden, swift growth of a party with the pretty name Golden Dawn. Its base is a band of pro-Nazi thugs. Tiny and hardly known before the crisis, it dawned upon the scene with amazing strength, winning 21 seats in the Greek legislature.

Before this swift prominence its leading man, Nikolaos Michaloliakos, had written: "We are the faithful soldiers of the National Socialist idea and nothing else" and "We exist and continue the battle for the final victory of our race... With our thoughts and soul devoted to the memory of our great Leader, we raise our right hand, salute the sun and, with courage impelled by our military honor and National Socialist duty we shout, full of passion, faith in the future and our visions: HEIL HITLER!"

The members still demonstrate this faith by raising their arms in Nazi salutes on every occasion.

That is not all they learned from Hitler. Their record of violence and murder is horrendous, directed against leftists and, above all, immigrants. Nationalist, chauvinist, racist hatred and brutality, especially against people of color, is their main occupation, along with vote-getting food handouts - insultingly restricted to "people of pure Greek background."

As in most countries, but especially Greece, sections of the police at all levels are supportive of the right, refraining from protecting victims of their thuggery, helping them to escape and hide when they are undeniably identified and even lending them batons and radio equipment during attacks on left-wing rallies. Many policemen vote for them, many young policemen are their recruits. This friendly relationship extends into the government, where several known fascists got high posts.

But when a Golden Dawn goon murdered a popular anti-fascist rapper, 50,000 marched in protest in Athens, and others in many cities of Greece and as far as Barcelona, Spain. The prime minister found it necessary to arrest many Golden Dawn leaders, some clearly implicated in the killing, and including members of the legislature, like party boss Michaloliakos. An investigation found that law enforcement officials had helped train the Golden Dawn paramilitary wing; eleven police officers, some of high rank, were fired or had to quit.

154 Strategy, Austerity, War and the Right

No trials have been held as yet, the status of Golden Dawn is unclear, and so is the number of delegates - if any - they can send in the Greek group of 21 EU delegates.

Hungary

Equally frightening and even stronger is Jobbik in Hungary. Officially the Movement for a Better Hungary, the name Jobbik, an acronym of its original title, Right-Wing Youth Association, is also a pun meaning something like "better go right". Founded by Catholic and Protestant university students as "a principled, conservative, radically patriotic Christian party ... to protect Hungarian values and interests," others describe it as fascist, neo-Nazi, extremist, racist, anti-Semitic, anti-Roma and homophobic.

Since inland Hungary does not have large numbers of refugees from Africa or Asia to attack, the fascists seek domestic prey. Its population of close to 10 million includes 50,000 to 100,000 Jews and 700,000 to 800,000 Roma people ("Gypsies"). The latter, the poorest group, are the fascists' main target. Again and again Jobbik utilizes local disputes or its own provocations to send gangs, mostly young men, to terrorize Roma communities, sometimes inflicting severe casualties. "Not all Gypsy people are criminals," Jobbik avers, but "certain specific criminological phenomena are predominantly and overwhelmingly" associated with the Roma minority. To solve "one of the severest problems facing Hungarian society", Jobbik proposed the creation of "public order zones ... sealing off, registering and monitoring criminal elements", segregating Roma children by sending them to boarding schools, increasing the "deterrent power of tough punishment and long sentencing" with a strengthened police force and a return of the death penalty. When polls indicated a temporary drop in public support for Jobbik three years ago it renewed its campaign against Roma with rallies in villages across the country, often ending in violence.

Attacks were often carried out by a formation called Magyar Gárda, founded in 2007 by Jobbik leaders and similar to Nazi storm troopers, even in its uniforms. In 2009 some judges, remnants of a more moderate era, ruled it illegal, but with or without uniforms, it still makes itself felt.

The reactionary, authoritarian ruling party Fidesz with its wannabe dictator Viktor Orbán, has said little to all this. As one Green member of the small opposition stated, near-silence at national level allows Fidesz "to avoid confronting right-wing voters sympathetic to Jobbik whom they hope to keep in their camp." One poll found 60% of Hungarians agreeing that "the inclination to criminality is in the blood of Gypsies."

On the question of anti-Semitism, Jobbik is equally fascist though less violent - as yet. A newsletter edited by a Jobbik candidate for the EP included the sentence: "Given our current situation, anti-Semitism is not just our right, it is the duty of every Hungarian lover of his homeland, and we must prepare for armed battle against the Jews." A Jobbik deputy in parliament wanted a commemoration of the notorious anti-Semitic "blood libel" case of 1882 on trumped-up charges of "Jews murdering Hungarian children". I

n 2012 a leading Jobbik deputy publicized his speech saying it is "timely to tally up people of Jewish ancestry here, especially in Parliament and the government, who indeed pose a national security risk to Hungary." The other parties, also the ruling Fidesz, vigorously denounced this and Jewish organizations called it a reintroduction of Nazism in the Parliament. But Viktor Orbán remains cautious; he dislikes unfavorable international attention, but then he also wants those votes. During attempts to erect statues idolizing the pro-fascist head of state Horthy and his government (1920-1944), Orbán tried to avoid taking any position.

Like most rightist parties, Jobbik loudly opposes the EU, building on popular views ranging from apathy or skepticism to hatred of "the slave-drivers in Brussels". Skepticism is more than appropriate, but for very different reasons, and meanwhile Jobbik takes part in EP elections. In 2009, with a surprisingly high 14 percent, it won three of Hungary's 21 seats, and hopes for many more - to increase the status and strength of this sector of the EP. Jobbik and the Golden Dawn mob in Greece are probably the most rabid and most openly fascist.

Bulgaria

The fourth largest party in Bulgaria is Ataka (Attack), formed in 2005 by Volen Siderov, a man who supports all kinds of positions: a rejection of NATO and US bases in Bulgaria, denunciation of world big business, support for popular measures like a minimum wage to raise the lowest living standard in the EU. But along with such demands are vicious attacks against a century-old Turkish community which is about eight percent of the population. Siderov insists that Turkey wants to seize Bulgaria and he and his followers loudly demand a ten billion dollar indemnity from Turkey because of alleged genocide during the Second Balkan War of 1913. Siderov claims that a secret, underground Free Mason conspiracy controls anti-Bulgarian governments everywhere. His party, which maintains a private TV channel, is close to the right-wing Orthodox Church and wants to increase church influence in all walks of life, especially the schools, eliminating all Islamic rights. Siderov's Ataka group favors a very controversial second atomic power plant in Bulgaria.

Sweden

The Sweden Democrats (Sverigedemokraterna, SD), founded in 1988 with aid from the French Front National, was at first openly fascist. Its members were photographed wearing Nazi uniforms. One leader had been an SS member and another was convicted for illegal possession of firearms and threatening to burn a Jewish actor, whom he called a "Jew pig". There were other scandals; an SD member of Parliament said two immigrants had thrown him from his wheelchair and stolen his backpack but it was found that he had left it in a restaurant and the immigrants had helped him back into his wheel chair after a fall. About the year 2000, the party decided to become more respectable and gained influence. But it remained sharply anti-Islamic, urging immigrants to "go home", and tried to weaken the rights of the Sami people in the North (the "Lapps"). Calling itself a "socially conservative party with a nationalist foundation" it remained far-right but not a fascist party.

Denmark

These events in Sweden seemed far too liberal to some Danes. The Danish People's Party, while calling for better welfare benefits and money for schools and environmental improvements, stresses its support for "family, the monarchy and the Church of Denmark" and, with its anti-immigrant and Islamophobic attacks, attracts many working people away from the Social Democrats.

This has made it so strong (or the others so weak) that its support was sought by the Conservative and Liberal parties for their minority coalition government led by Anders Fogh Rasmussen, now Secretary General of NATO. They were untroubled by its extreme views and its sharp rejection of even the vague moderation of Sweden's rightist party, as displayed sarcastically by its founder and long-time leader Pia Kjærsgaard who said: "If they want to turn (Swedish) Stockholm, Gothenburg or Malmö into a Scandinavian Beirut, with clan wars, honor killings and gang rapes, let them do it. We can always put a barrier on the (connecting) Øresund Bridge."

Norway

The situation in Norway is similar. The Progress Party, despite its name, is just as anti-immigrant and Islamophobic but, like the Swedish Party, tries to avoid obviously extreme positions. It has developed ties to the Tories in Britain and Republicans in the USA (often leaning in a "libertarian" Tea Party direction). And it is very willing to join a coalition government with Norwegian Conservatives.

Belgium

Vlaams Belang (VB) means "Flemish Interest". The party claims to protect language and culture of the Dutch-speaking majority in the Flanders region of Belgium against the minority Walloons in the south and in the capital, Brussels, who speak French. Indeed, it advocates a break-away, in other words independence. It is also against immigrants, especially if they are Muslims. Its predecessor, Vlaams Blok, was barred by court order in 2004 because of its nasty racism, whereupon its leader reconstituted it under a new name, with less virulent-sounding policies, but stated, "We change our name, but not our tricks. We change our name, but not our program." Now it calls for repatriation only of those immigrants who "reject, deny or combat" Flemish culture and "certain European values, including freedom of expression, equality between men and women", while women who wear the hijab veil have "effectively signed their contract for deportation." Despite words on freedom and equality, it is described as very far right. And in Flanders it is very popular!

One aspect is of special interest. This party, no longer viewed as anti-Semitic, has developed ties to the large Jewish community of Antwerp, traditionally based on diamond-cutting, and now sees Jews and Israel as allies against Islam. Such unexpected ties are not restricted to VB. In 2010 its representative, known for contacts with SS veterans, joined a Swedish Democrat, a far-right German and Heinz-Christian Strache, head of the Austrian Freedom Party, in a friendship visit to Israel. Strache, with notorious ties to Austrian neo-Nazis and Holocaust deniers, donned an Israeli Defense Forces combat jacket and camouflage paint while visiting paratroopers near the Gaza Strip.

After visiting Yad Vashem the group drove past Palestinian villages to a West Bank Jewish settlement, one of many it found necessary to defend Israel against its enemies. Later, members of the Knesset welcomed the visitors: Nissim Zeev from the Orthodox right-wing party Shas said, "At the end of the day what's important is their attitude - the fact they really love Israel." Likud member Kara, a deputy prime minister, told journalists: "Israel needs friends: Strache might be the next Austrian chancellor." In a "Jerusalem Declaration" the men stated: "We stand at the vanguard in the fight for the Western, democratic community" against the "totalitarian threat" of "fundamentalist Islam."

Australian writer Antony Loewenstein, commenting on the visit, wrote: "Yesterday's anti-Semites have reformed themselves as today's crusading heroes against an unstoppable Muslim birth rate on a continent that now sees Islam as an intolerant and ghettoized religion." And it would seem that that some on the Jewish right can forget the past and greet the political offspring of those who once so tragically used Jews as scape-goats - and now employ the same old methods.

Germany

What about those offspring in their old Vaterland? The National Dem-ocratic Party of Germany (NPD), the most important neo-Nazi party since 1945, has grown and ebbed. It grew when East Germany was hitched to the Federal Republic. With its industry and much of its agriculture dismantled, with millions suddenly disoriented politically and young people vainly seeking meaning or hope in life, skilled agi-tators from the West and new ones from the East had good hunting grounds.

The NPD has hardly concealed ties to violent anti-foreigner, anti-leftist gangs - and to sympathetic officials. An effort to outlaw the NPD failed in 2003 and a new attempt is dragging on.

A five percent minimum vote is needed to send deputies to the national Bundestag or state legislatures, thus keeping the NPD out in all but two East German states, Saxony and Mecklenburg-West Pomerania. But this restriction does not apply to European Parliament elections, so the NPD is in the race with its vicious anti-foreigner, especially anti-Roma post-ers. Many other small or splinter parties will also try, on the right, on the left or with special agendas - from ecology to senior rights. They will run, but few will win even single seats.

One party, founded last year, missed the five percent needed for the Bundestag but could well win a seat or two in the EP. The main plank of this Alternative for Germany (AfD) is opposition, not to the EU (at least in its statements) but to the euro currency.

Otherwise it remains much of a puzzle, with anti-foreigner positions represented if not dominant. Its surprising resonance (4 to 6 percent) is a result of widespread feelings of apathy or hostility toward the EU, fanned, as in most countries, by nationalist media. It is uncertain how the AfD will develop and with whom it will align.

The EP now has seven groups or caucuses, from left to right. Caucuses receive funds, rooms and committee rights but must have at least 25 more or less compatible members from at least seven countries. The UKIP and the now greatly weakened Northern League of Italy were in one such group; most rightists remained independent. Now there will certainly be a new right-wing caucus, possibly excluding the most rabid (Jobbik, Golden Dawn and NDP) but extremely menacing all the same.

The Left

And will there be no left-wing opposition?

There was indeed a group on the left - with an unwieldy title: European United Left/Nordic Green Left (GUE/NGL). (Nordic means Scandinavian here.) Most of the 19 member organizations from 14 countries are also members of the closely-related Party of the European Left, but some belong to the anti-EU, more radical European Anti-Capitalist Left. Of those in the EP group till now five were Communist parties, from France, Portugal, Greece and Czechoslovakia, two were Trotskyist, from Ireland and France, some call themselves Socialist. There are sometimes two parties from one country, often differing sharply, as with the Greek Communists (KKE) and Syriza. Some members sharply oppose the European Union but take part all the same. The group also includes two delegates from the Harmony Center of Latvia, a party of the Russian-speaking minority, and one from Sinn Fein in Northern Ireland. Best represented were Czechoslovakia (4 seats), Portugal and Greece (5 each), France (6) and the German LINKE with 8. The others had only one or two seats. For chairperson Gabi Zimmer from the LINKE the job was often like herding cats. Amazingly, she survived; they even won a few skirmishes for good causes.

But now the deck will be reshuffled. There are hopes for more left-wing members, especially from Greece due to the growth of Syriza, whose head, Alexis Tsipras, is the candidate of the European Left Party to chair the European Commission in Brussels. He is popular among many leftists but the likely winner for that job in Brussels will be the German Social Democrat Martin Schulz.

Although the LINKE of Germany will probably retain more or less its present strength, it too varies in its views. Especially those further to the left, more numerous in West Germany than in former GDR states, are critical of the entire EU mission for reasons indicated at the beginning of this article.

At a recent congress on the campaign program, these critics wanted to include a description of the EU as "neo-liberal (here like neo-conservative), militaristic and largely undemocratic". The so-called "reformers" were able to talk them out of it; the words did not seem conducive to winning apathetic supporters to go to the EU polls and vote for the LINKE. There was also a compromise on choosing candidates for the election; of the ten with any chance of winning, five were from the east, five from the west, five were women, five men, with a somewhat similar split on varying outlooks. A sort of unity was achieved.

A major party congress May 10-11, after this article has been sent off, may or may not ease differences, or sharpen them. They are based on the question, recurring in so many left-wing movements, as to how much the Left should participate in the on-going political system. Should it stress achievable improvements for the majority of the people, trying to increase its influence while even joining Social Democrats or Greens in occasional coalitions, if at the price of some compromises, and thus basically accepting the status quo at least for now?

Or should it stress its opposition to the whole system, putting its goal of replacing capitalism at the center of its demands? Can the struggle against the menace of bloody conflict - now so threatening, unite the two sides? Or the necessity to fight the dangerous strength of rabid re-actionaries, using a hatred of minorities to win over working people who once listened far more closely to the Left? The response to such fateful questions will play a role at the coming party congress of the LINKE. It will also influence the future of the European Union and, as we see in the Ukraine, in the street of Venezuela, the ruins of Syria and elsewhere - the future far beyond the shores of this smallish continent.

'The Desperate Encounter..."

Greg King, a CCDSer and trade unionist, died April 18, 2014 at age 63 after a brief illness. He was a graduate of Boston Latin school, the University of Hawaii and held a master's degree from Boston College. He is survived by his loving wife Supron Phasang and his siblings Ellenmarie Evins of Short Hills, NJ Jane King of Boston and Fred King of Chicopee, MA and many other family members. An extended obituary is at the website of his union, seiu888.org. Following is a short essay he wrote in his final months.

By Greg King

Quite a few years ago, I read everything by the late French philosopher, essayist Albert Camus, as translated into English, that I could get my hands on. As it turned out, that was exactly the wrong time of my life to be reading what can be overwhelmingly depressive stuff.

Well, now I think I have arrived at the right time, not because of the depressive aspects of Camus, but rather because of a newly discovered ("Light shines on Marblehead") kernel of humanism and hope, to be found among all the outwardly negative writing.

Camus does affirm, in particular in what I am rereading now, The Rebel, but also in wonderful books like The Plague and The First Man, as well as essays like The Myth of Sisyphus, a life-affirming raison d'etre, so to speak.

On rereading The Rebel, I came upon passages which speak right to me and my situation now. Passages like " - - - the desperate encounter between human inquiry and the silence of the universe - - - ."

It is a desperate encounter when one is searching for answers and hope, and one only hears the deafening roar of silence. I'd say we each must look within our own selves, compare what we find with others, discuss our common circumstances with others, and act in life from that point.

Remember in G.W.F. Hegel's Phenomenology of the Spirit, the Master and the Slave confront each other, hate each other, until they each notice their own reflections in each other's eyes. Then they develop self-respect, re-spect for the "Other" and develop a more unified, humanistic perspective.

I know I'm really stretching what's to be found in that part of the Phe-nomenology. I know I'm making it sort of namby-pamby and finding universality where none exists. However, what does not exist should be brought into being, if our actions and sentiments coincide.

This is a world filled with poverty, oppression, keeping-folks-in-igno-rance, a near-total lack of compassion, tolerance and sense of justice, right here in Boston, as in so many other places. It doesn't have to stay that way, though. Talk to your sisters and brothers, as we do every day as labor activists, anyway. Learn their thoughts. Share yours. You know the two or more of you can develop a common perspective, though of course not always.

One of my favorite quotes of all time is martyred South African anti-apartheid activist , Steve Biko, saying, "The most powerful weapon in the hands of the oppressor is the mind of the oppressed." Free your minds. Free your children's minds. Education, as well as gumption, is one of the few ways out of working people's dilemmas.

"Teach your children well. Their father's [and mother's] hell will slowly go by." All of us have a tool within us to fight back against oppression and injustice. That tool is the realization, reached sooner or later, that we each are worthy of respect and the accordance of dignity. If we don't have those, we should stand up, speak up, and demand them.

Camus's one time friend and later bitter enemy, Jean-Paul Sartre, said such things as, "Existence precedes essence" and "We create our lives through our deeds." I really believe that. I have since I picked up one of my sister's textbooks, while she attended the old Boston State Teachers College, read it and thought about it.

Your own lives may have turned in different directions. Rejoice in them, celebrate them, but keep your mind open to considering other beliefs, other perspectives. As Ben Franklin or someone like him said, "We must all hang together, or we'll all hang separately."

There IS a "desperate encounter between human inquiry and the silence of the universe." Listen to "the sounds of silence," and find the answers in your own hearts, as well as those of your sisters and brothers with whom you mutually develop a common perspective.

We're all in this together. Nobody has the right to claim all the luxury seats. We have to go out and fight for what is rightfully ours.

The Lost Writings of SDS...A New Collection Edited by Carl Davidson

Revolutionary Youth & the New Working Class

The Praxis Papers, the Port Authority Statement, the RYM Documents and Other Lost Writings of SDS

Edited by Carl Davidson

This is a fascinating new collection of 12 essays and documents from the New Left of the late 1960s, gathered and commented on by Carl Davidson, a national leader of SDS at the time.

'Revolutionary Youth and the New Working Class' contains key sources illuminating a critical transition period in the American left, as well as a number of ideas still relevant.

Most important is the 'Port Authority Statement', actually titled 'Toward a Theory of Social Change,' and written by Robert Gottlieb, Gerry Tenney and David Gilbert. Passed around in mimeographed form, only about a third of it was ever put into print in SDS's newspaper, until factional struggles set it aside. Meant to replace the Port Huron Statement, it is remarkable for many insights still holding up today.

The collection includes other 'Praxis Papers,' including three by Davidson, the Revolutionary Youth Movement documents that replied to the Weatherman faction, and the original 'White Blindspot' documents. About half the content has been scattered across the internet, but much of it has been newly digitized and now available in both e-book and paperback form from Changemaker Publications. Go to the site for the full contents, and contact the editor at carld717@gmail.com for bulk rates.

To see the full contents go to http://www.lulu.com/product/paperback/revolutionary-youth-and-the-new-working-class/17144702 and click 'preview' under the picture of the cover

The 'Lone Ranger' Period Is Over! We Need You to Join Us....

We're inviting you to join the Committees of Correspondence for Democracy and Socialism. We need your help in building a progressive majority for peace, justice and equally—and then pushing on to a new society where these will be the rule, rather than the exception. Socialism is being more widely discussed today than any time since the 1960s, and you can't take part in it fully without a socialist organization.

Working with many others, CCDS aims to end existing wars and prevent new ones. We oppose the current austerity being imposed upon the working people, a burden made even heavier by militarism and the hidden costs of non-renewable energy systems. We need a global order based on peaceful relations among nations, mutual respect and human rights, and the creation of economies that can exist in harmony with nature.

You can make a difference. Lend a hand in organizing with others to fight for a progressive agenda in the streets, workplaces, communities of faith and schools. It's not crowded up front, so sign up today!

Fill out and mail today.
_____ Yes, I'd like to join the CCDS. Enclosed is my check for:
$ _____.
  I'd like a subscription to Dialogue & Initiative. Enclosed is my check for $12.50 (Non-Members, $15.00).
  I know good causes need money. Here is my contribution of
$_____.

Name _____
Address _____
City _____ State _____ Zip _____
Phone_____ Email _____

Make check payable to Committees of Correspondence, and mail to: CCDS Membership, 6422 Irwin Ct., Oakland, CA, 94609

Email: national@cc-ds.org Web: www.cc-ds.org

The Committees of Correspondence for Democracy and Socialism (CCDS) is a national organization dedicated to the struggle for justice, equality, democracy, peace and socialism. The annual membership is $36 for individuals; $18 for unemployed, seniors, youth, and others with low income; $48 for households

Online University of the Left

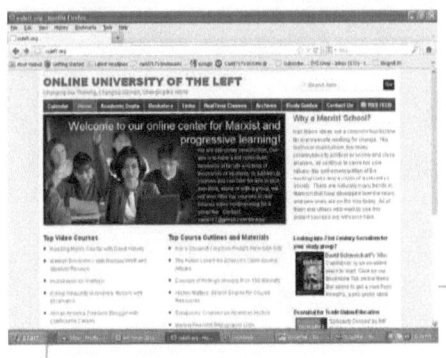

Study! Teach! Organize!

We are a free and open university with all the diverse views on the left. We are inspired by Karl Marx, whose ideas are a common touchstone for many people working for change. His historical materialism, his many contributions to political economy and class analysis, all continue to serve our core values--the self-emancipation of the working class and a vision of a classless society. There are naturally many trends in Marxism that have developed over the years, and new ones are on the rise today. All of them, and other radicals and progressives who want to see this project succeed, are welcome here.

- Free political and cultural programming with hundreds of video classes

- Ideal for book store programs, book promotions & study groups

- Faculty: get 'double duty' out of your online materials by placing them here as well

- Course outlines & in-depth text archives; use for teach-ins. Just get a projector and a screen!

- Coming soon! Interactive classes in real time for a small fee.

- Speakers also available

- Your input & feedback is welcome! Use our Facebook page, too!

http://ouleft.org

A Left Unity Project of the Committees of Correspondence for Democracy and Socialism
Http://cc-ds.org To get involved, contact: Carl Davidson at carld717@gmail.com

npliance